D1459651

Doctor Morrison's Amazing Healing Foods: With Miracle Health Promoter M

Other Books by Marsh Morrison

*Doctor Morrison's Miracle Body Tune-Up for
Rejuvenated Health
Doctor Morrison's Miracle Guide to Pain-Free
Health and Longevity*

Doctor Morrison's Amazing Healing Foods: With Miracle Health Promoter M

Marsh Morrison
D.C., Ph.C., F.I.C.C.

Parker Publishing Company, Inc.
West Nyack, New York

Library of Congress Cataloging in Publication Data

Morrison, Marsh.
  Doctor Morrison's Amazing healing foods.

  Includes index.
  1. Diet therapy. 2. Vegetarianism. I. Title
II. Title: Amazing healing foods.
RM217.M63   615.8'54   81-14202
ISBN 0-13-217125-2   AACR2

Printed in the United States of America

DEDICATION

TO MY LOVELY LADY
Who fired me and inspired me

How You May Reasonably Expect This Book to Healthify You

This book is almost extravagantly full of good, natural, *tested* health-restoring things to help you. This is said with barely any qualification, for it applies to nearly any condition or ailment that may bother you.

After more than fifty years of doctoring with a method that understands the overuse and abuse of both drugs and surgery, and depending on neither in my practice, I am loath to declare any state of disease absolutely incurable. Why so? Because the way people with all kinds of ailments have responded to the treatments set forth in this book has made me realize that there is hardly any incurable malady but only wrong and unnatural treatment programs for ailments called incurable. So long as people live and breathe, so long as their hair and fingernails grow, so long as there remains some life in the organism, I have found that there is some chance of improvement if not full recovery. This is so because of two reasons: First, because nature tends toward the normal—note how the body fairly yearns to heal every cut and bruise without the need of any doctor's diagnosis; and secondly, if the healthifying programs are natural and right, as they are in these pages, the body returns to a state of wellness in almost every case, no matter how irremediable other doctors have called the condition.

What faced me in writing a good, useful, helpful book of this kind was this: Do I merely set forth what to do that is almost immediately beneficial for any condition, or do I explain *why* you ought to do what I tell you to do?

There are arguments on both sides. Some readers favor both approaches. The philosopher Plato wrote that to give sick people reasons why is almost trying to make doctors of them, but sick people do not desire by way of education to be made doctors but only to be made well. From my experience as a teacher of doctors, however, I have reason to value knowing the why of things.

Rules can be forgotten and often are. But if you know why a thing should be done, you then needn't bother about rules because understanding the reason tells you what the rule should be.

Consider this simple example. *Don't go swimming soon after eating.* That's the rule. But here's the *why* of it. When food is in the stomach the blood is drawn towards the digestive organs in order to start cooking down (digesting) the food to its end products. If you jump right into vigorous swimming, or into a hot bath, the blood is drawn off to the muscles for its activity, or to the skin surface, away from the digestive organs. Lacking enough blood to power its job, the stomach slows down, the food sours, there's belching and burping and a whole chain of ensuing problems along the entire gastrointestinal line. So one should do what animals do after a meal: curl up and nap, or rest. This permits the digestive apparatus to make full use of the blood for its work, whereas swimming or bathing tends to draw away the needed blood. Now you know the reason why it is wrong to be active after a meal, and you don't need to remember the exact rule. My way of putting it to student doctors in my college classes was this: "One reason why is worth a hundred rules."

So in this book I do both. Where it is important, I spell out the reason why. Mostly, however, I simply tell you what to do for your illness, not why you must do it.

If you have a heart ailment you'll find in these pages exactly the Amazing Healing Foods that act somewhat like drugs for the heart would—only better because they are natural, with no side effects. And to make sure that such restorative foods are assimilated, you will learn the precise manner of applying the Miracle Health Promoter M, which makes healing come about. If you suffer from distressing heart pains you'll find here the foods that will usually still such pains and do it safely, plus, as in all cases, the Miracle Health Promoter M to make it all work.

Whether yours be an ailment of the heart or lungs or kidneys or whatever, in this book you will find a two-pronged benefit in the shape of (1) case histories of others with similar conditions who gained and maintained health through these programs, and (2) the oft-mentioned Miracle Health Promoter M, which constitutes thoroughly tested body movements that tend to correct pinched nerves, replace the body in proper structural alignment, and thus set up an uninterrupted flow of life force nerve power that assures the utilization of the amazing healing foods, for, if any potentially valuable foods do not reach the cells, they're not actually valuable and it is as though one hadn't eaten them.

In the following pages there are foods that improve one's sex drive; remarkable foods that almost miraculously help in brain fatigue and memory lapses; amazing foods to heal and strengthen the lungs and bronchial tubes; miracle foods for relieving digestive disorders; well-tested foods for aiding a poorly functioning liver, and for beneficially energizing a malfunctioning pancreas, weak kidneys, and incontinent urinary bladder, and many other surprisingly effective foods that tend to heal and restore and normalize almost every other organ of the body much more quickly and far more safely than anything presently known in the pharmacological manuals. And, most importantly—and absolutely unique to this book of get-well pages—the assurance in all cases of using the Miracle Health Promoter M that makes renewed, rejuvenated health possible.

This amazing, newer knowledge of nutrition and miracle health promoter factor was derived from 102 independent research projects conducted under proper control conditions over a span of fifty years, and not conducted under the restraints of, or obligated to, the American Medical Association, medical societies, or pharmaceutical interests. Triggering every one of the

102 researches was the need to discover how to be healthy in an unhealthy world. And the meaty middle of what I know or have learned is in this book.

Where my findings differ from the so-called "medical wisdoms," I found my approaches right and the medical ones wrong; no wonder that despite all the research millions lavished on them they are still behind the ever-rising incidence of heart disease, cancer, mental illness, diabetes, arthritis, emphysema, epilepsy, renal dysfunctions, and the rest. Mere millions alone, or impressive research equipment, will not conquer diseases where the approach and fundamental starting premises are physiologically inexact.

Besides the amazing healing foods for the conditions mentioned above, these pages contain lists of the remarkable "food medicines" that aid the uterus and cure its functional discomforts, that tend to restore the power of the prostate gland, that frequently rehabilitate arthritic joints, that recondition human skin and hair, that very often mend nerve damage; also seven foods for visual health, and three outstanding throat healthifying foods, and so on and on—all of these in addition to the simple, but simply amazing, structural self-aligning instructions which make the Miracle Health Promoter M.

The foods we deal with here are common foods, not the uncommon or hard-to-get variety, usually. Almost always they are foods that can add ten years to your life, and life to your ten years.

Every important health aid of valuable significance that I have researched in over half a century of doctoring and researching is in this book. This is my twenty-ninth book. If one seeking my advice had only enough spending money for just one of my books, it is this one that I would without hesitation counsel him to read and heed. This is so because within these pages almost anyone who is plagued with virtually any illness may reasonably expect to learn how to regain, and then maintain, a precious, desirable level of health.

Marsh Morrison
Tucson, Arizona

Table of Contents

Doctor Morrison's Amazing Healing Foods: With Miracle Health Promoter M

1

Foods That Build Up the Heart

All of us know that we are creatures of habit. What is not so well understood is that we are just as much creatures of good habits as of bad ones.

Getting used to a good habit, such as eating foods that are physiologically acceptable and therapeutically good for the heart, can stick with you all the remaining days and years of your life.

In this book, beginning right now, we launch ourselves into becoming slaves of good habits—like the habit of consuming plentifully of what is good for the heart—just as we became victims of bad habits in the past.

Of chief importance as a healing food for the heart is wheat germ. It is plentiful, it is cheap, it is one of the best protein items of nutrition available on this planet. Most protein foods are expensive: note the cost tickets attached to steaks, fresh fish, processed cheeses. Yet wheat germ, which is far more beneficial a protein foodstuff for weak and ailing hearts than any of the others, is as inexpensive as any reasonable person might desire. A full pound of it sells for under a dollar, and a pound supplies nutrition of the finest kind for many days.

There are other good protein foods, as we shall see in the pages ahead. But wheat germ is not only the best protein as a *protein;* as a miracle longevity food for the heart it leads all others by a wide margin. The other "heart foods," as we shall soon learn, are excellent sources of nutrition while secondary as heart-healing foods. Wheat germ ranks almost alone because of the sound physiological reason that it is, in a very real sense, a specific for the heart. Thus it is the best of the good ones.

THE MAGIC OF WHEAT GERM

What is there about this food that makes it so specifically a healing food for the heart? Here we must understand what usually happens in a stricken heart and what there is in wheat germ to alleviate or overcome the trouble. I refer to an ingredient known technically as d-alpha tocopherol. This is a fine inner ingredient of wheat germ, a part of the vitamin E factor within wheat germ.

Medically, a heart patient suffering from coronary artery disease or other cardiac problems is given daily blood-thinning drug. This is needed because the heart patient's blood tends to clot and interfere with the flow of blood nutrition to the heart. The drug is taken specifically to prevent clotting and thus keep the supply lines of blood to the heart muscle open and unimpeded.

In wheat germ, it is the d-alpha portion that keeps human blood thinned down naturally, safely, effectively. A small daily cereal bowl of wheat germ with skim milk is beautifully protective for cardiac victims, and without an iota of side effects ever, at any time. This is because the d-alpha content of wheat germ is the body's *natural* anti-clotting substance.

Medical legend has it that the principal cause of death in America is coronary artery disease, commonly called coronary occlusion. In my own research projects done on an independent level, not indebted to the American Medical Association or medical societies or pharmaceutical interests, I have come up with findings and answers to dispute this, but that is a matter to be taken up elsewhere. For now, suffice to say that coronary occlusion is an arterial problem wherein the vessels that convey blood to the heart (usually two of them, sometimes three) become occluded or clotted with plaques. These plaques constitute a kind of sludge somewhat the consistency of toothpaste, and they hang onto the inner walls of the arteries, thus making the arterial passageway smaller. If you have ever seen a water pipe encrusted with lime or other debris that narrows the inside area of the pipe, you can imagine a coronary artery with much the same situation.

My own displeasure with medical anti-coagulant drugs prescribed by medical doctors in heart cases is that they produce side effects as do all drugs, including aspirin and other common medicines that American people have come to take unthinkingly just as though they were popping peanuts into the mouth. You must understand clearly what side effects really mean, for they are unutterably serious and have caused a pileup of diseases in the land beyond calculation.

Side effects are effects in the body *besides* what the body suffered before taking the drugs. Side effects are effects within the system in addition to the maladies already existing. As one writer put it, "A drug with side effects, and hardly any are without side effects, leaves two diseases in the body where but a single disease existed before." So you can understand why this author feels so keenly enthusiastic about a food such as wheat germ that is not only a first-rate miracle longevity food for the heart, but does not have even the faintest scintilla of side effects.

Drugs have the habit of building physiological and pathological troubles in the human organism—one of those bad habits I mentioned. Many diseases that plague the nation today have come to be called iatrogenic (physician-caused) ailments. A favorite medicine taken by millions to suppress the symptoms of a cold is one I strike out against with some fury exactly because it does that: it suppresses what ought to be sneezed or coughed or sweated out of the body, leaving the poisons to be accumulated and build new diseases within the system. But none of this occurs with wheat germ, the purest kind of food which is also an anti-coagulant without being a drug.

In this imperfect world there are not too many items of nutrition with natural healing ingredients built into the food. If you will remember that there are no side effects from a food, but only from a drug, and that wheat germ has this drug-like anti-clotting and heart-helping quality as a natural built-in ingredient, then, since you now understand what side effects truly mean, you will favor wheat germ with an enthusiasm that equals my own.

There are other foods that I have found specifically good for the heart. While wheat germ is the one I consider most important for extending life through improved cardiovascular function, one cannot forever eat just wheat germ. To know the other "heart helpers" is to have a good handy armamentarium at hand. Before going into these other good heart fuel foods, and just how to prepare and combine all the heart-healing food items into palatable dishes, I must tell you about the case of little Gregory.

Here was a chubby boy of almost 11 who had a sad history of rheumatic heart disease. He weighed 80 pounds, had very little immunity or resistance against infections because of a suspected thymus dysfunction, suffered from labored breathing and could not play with other boys since a bout with rheumatic fever four years earlier. The parents were wealthy and took Greg around unstintingly to what they denominated "the best cardiologists," but still the boy wheezed and was listless and overate, while almost wholly inactive.

Fortunately, he liked a large cereal dish at breakfast. There I could employ wheat germ advantageously, but in small meals because my researches had established beyond doubt that cardiac patients needed a few small meals rather than three heaping "squares" a day. Also, I found the cardiologists' exercise program for the boy quite wrong. I put the boy on two bathroom scales with his little feet equidistantly apart, one foot on each, and instead of his weighing 40 pounds on each scale he was 32 pounds on one side and 48 on the other, a fact that showed he was exhaustingly offside and had to use up his strength to fight staying in balance like a car that had been in a collision and dragged offside as one drove it.

I explained to Greg's father and mother two matters of great importance. One, that he was structurally out of alignment and no machine that was out of balanced adjustment could reasonably be expected to function normally. Two, that while his heart doctor was right in recommending an exercise program for the boy, it was just exactly wrong to do any physical drills standing and sitting straight up in defiance of gravity when the heart was already weak and should not be required to pump more blood faster to the child's distal extremities straight uphill. They understood at once the wisdom of slowly building strength into the heart muscle through exercises, but exercises done on the floor or bed while the heart was on the same level as the body and could pump out the blood accelerated through exercise without hurtful strain. Also they understood that the potential value of any food is not its actual value—and this needs a bit of explaining.

Even the best foods, those of great potential usefulness, first must be appropriated by the body, absorbed and metabolized and utilized before their potential values to the body become actual values. If there are misalignments that prevent the flow of vital life forces to the digestive apparatus, for example, proper conversion cannot take place because along with the mechanical misalignments there are nerve pressures which prevent the free flow of life force to the digestive organs. This explains why some sick folk always buy the most natural and health-promising foods in expensive health food stores and forever remain sick. It is because they are out of mechanical adjustment usually. They have interfering pressures on nerve pathways that must deliver power and direction to their digestive apparatus. Lacking such power, even the potentially best foods fail to become converted and utilized, remaining potentially valuable rather than actually valuable to the ailing body.

Here is a lesson I shall repeat many times in the pages ahead with reference to healing foods for other organs and other ailments: namely, that to ensure the best use and utilization of amazing healing foods the body must at the same time be in somewhat correct alignment, not in a state of maladjustment. I never tire of getting this truth across in all my writing: a machine such as the human body, which is made up of many movable mechanical parts, when out of mechanical adjustment cannot work right until put back into a mechanically aligned state.

I explained to Greg's parents the value of wheat germ. I emphasized that the grain must be fresh, for rancid wheat germ, as with all grains, can even cause stomach cancer. The way to avoid rancidity is merely to smell the container before taking out the wheat germ; if it's rancid your nose will tell you at once.

To put the child's body into a mechancially correct state so that it could assimilate all the health-giving value of wheat germ, I laid out a proper exercise program that was fun to the boy.

First, he was amazed that he weighed 16 pounds more on his left side than his right. I told him to race on his hands and knees on the lawn of his house, to do it without shoes so that his bare feet could contact Mother Earth, and to do it mornings when there might be dew on the grass. Fortunately, his family had an estate-like place where he could race on hands and knees on their own grassy knolls. I explained to Greg that only human beings insulate themselves from the fine emanations of the earth with shoes, and he nodded understandingly. Then I had a dialogue with the 11-year-old.

BECOME A DEPUTY DOCTOR

"You know what a deputy sheriff is, don't you, Greg?" I asked. Of course he did from seeing all those Westerns. "Well, I want you to become a deputy doctor," I added.

His job was simple and he was enthusiastic. Every morning he was to stand on the two simple bathroom scales and write down his weight on both sides. Then he was to put on his knees the foam rubber pads his mother had cut out for him and race on hands and knees on the lawn until somewhat tired. Finally, he was to recheck his weight on the scales and determine if his racing across the lawn changed anything; that is, whether it brought him more nearly into mechanical balance or possibly even widened the difference in his left and right side weights.

"One thing more, Gregory," I said. "In the cool of the evening each day I want you to ride your bike until you get a little tired, then check your weight on the two scales and write down, as an assistant research doctor should, if the bike riding or the hands-and-knees races make more of a difference in your lopsidedness."

He agreed avidly, smiling broadly and importantly. I had in mind changing to other activities if these two did not help put his small, but chubby body back into adjustment.

As it happened, along with the amazing healing foods I recommended, everything came right and he needed no further exercise program. The lad had a daily schedule in which he importantly participated, and he grew slimmer and firmer. His constant tiredness was replaced by an enthusiasm for activity in only a few weeks. He no longer became victim to every infection in the area and a workup, including a thymus test, showed improvement in the gland. Most noticeable of all, he no longer wheezed and his breathing was not a labored, difficult function. The latter was achieved by a bedtime diaphragmatic exercise I gave him to reoxygenate the system before he went to sleep. It consisted merely of raising his arms and panting like a dog, moving the great breathing muscle, the diaphragm, in and out as he panted, thus strengthening his chief organ of the breathing mechanism. The diaphragm, like all muscles, grows stronger with use and this in-and-out bedtime drill strengthened Gregory's breathing function in short order while at the same time oxygenating his little body for a good night's sleep.

Now—specifically—what were the miracle foods that did the job? Besides wheat germ I recommended a daily helping of the following secondary healing foods for the heart: blackstrap molasses, brown rice, raw pecan nuts, lecithin flakes (or liquid lecithin if tolerated), rice water as a daily drink in place of junk-food soda pops, bioflavonoids, either sunflower seeds or pumpkin seeds as a daily protein, and one egg every day, especially the yolk. And as in all cases, about 600 units of vitamin E every day.

The foregoing were daily items, more or less. Other secondary heart-healing items (secondary only to wheat germ, remember), could be taken every second or third day. These included yogurt, raw garlic, brewer's yeast, watermelon and whole wheat toast, the latter spread with blackstrap molasses.

Now follows the real crux of this chapter: that is, *why*—for what reason—are each of the aforementioned foods specifically heart-healing and generally health-improving items of nutrition? This is the part of the book you will remember, the part that will help you and your loved ones into natural health without resorting to drugs and their nasty, disease-making side effects.

First, however, a short paragraph as to why Gregory was so much offside as to weigh 32 pounds on one half of his little body and 48 on the other half. On inquiring and boring into the case history I extracted from his parents something they hadn't considered causative at all. At age seven, the child had gone on an old-fashioned hay ride in the country and Greg had fallen off the wagon onto the hard gravel road when the wagon jolted and the boy he was scuffling with let go. Greg complained of a bruised hip and the family medical doctor gave him a pain pill plus an injection into the buttock, just as though that could put back into adjustment the misalignment that the jarring fall had caused. In all my years as a doctor I have never seen a heart case of any kind that did not reveal upon careful examination an associated mechanical distortion that produced nerve pressures, which in turn robbed the heart muscle of its "working juice"—a free flow of nerve impulses. The conversation with Gregory's parents adduced the revealing information that soon after the fall from the hay wagon came the rheumatic fever that resulted in his having a rheumatic heart.

In this frame of reference, there was the elderly Mrs. Lawrence with her cardiac arrhythmia that always frightened her to death, making her think the next breath would be her last. In her case also there was a bodily jolt that preceded the heart trouble. While walking leisurely on the sidewalk, a teenaged lad on a bicycle came careening along and knocked the lady down, sending her sprawling on her face with a jolt that lacerated her elbows and broke her glasses. Soon after this she awoke with a pounding heart, then missing beats and an identifiable lack of rhythm in her heart sounds, all this not responding to the drugs prescribed by her medical man and getting worse until I saw her.

Near Mrs. Lawrence's home there were two streets on different levels connected by a steep line of stone steps, and she was told to do several daily turns at mounting and dismounting these steps while also taking long walks for her bulging varicose veins. Along with the foods I recommended for her heart, those I am about to explain in the following paragraphs, this elderly lady of 62 not only lost her distressing cardiac symptoms, but also the cosmetically annoying knots in her legs.

In first place, next to wheat germ, I must place lecithin because it also is a heart-feeding item that is at the same time a longevity food, one that tends to ensure a free and unobstructed flow of blood to the heart through unclotted coronary vessels.

What is most arresting about lecithin is that it is just as much a brain food of primary importance as it is a food for the entire cardiovascular system. You should be informed that almost one-fifth of your brain is made up of lecithin. It is a constituent of every cell and bone and organ and gland of your body. In the following chapter that deals with Eight Available Foods That Add Power to the Brain, I place lecithin first because its many "healthifying" qualities apply to heart tissues as well as to brain tissues. Here is an item of food that is almost as useful for extending brain health as heart life.

WHAT LECITHIN DOES

What lecithin does is this: in a graphic sense that is also scientifically valid, it rinses away the cholesterol deposits and plaques that block the coronary arteries and prevent a free flow of that blood to the heart which the heart muscle itself must have for its pumping action. In a mysterious way not fully understood, lecithin works at dissolving the arterial deposits that interfere with good, rich, oxygenated blood reaching the heart. In the brain, as will be made clear in the next chapter dealing with that organ, by dissolving the clotting plaques, lecithin makes it possible for a freer flow of blood that at once improves mental work, memory, general cerebral function.

Happily, many ordinary supermarkets carry lecithin flakes these days. In the case of the little boy Greg, with rheumatic heart disease, I advised adding about three tablespoonsful of lecithin flakes to this morning bowl of raw wheat germ and skim milk. When the cereal was also flavored with one tablespoonful of blackstrap molasses it constituted a powerful array of heart-fuel items that beat anything in pharmacology that I know about. But for a disciplined grown person who really desires fast results I recommend lecithin in its liquid form, available at health food stores. I say a "disciplined" person because lecithin has a somewhat disagreeable way of sticking to the roof of the mouth that children and many fussy oldsters cannot abide. In my own lifestyle I take a large spoonful of liquid lecithin every day at bedtime, missing only when away from home on a lecture tour.

THE WONDERS OF BLACKSTRAP MOLASSES

Reviewing blackstrap molasses is agreeable work, for this wonder-item of nutrition is exceedingly rich in potassium, among other goodies, and potassium extends life by giving life to a weak heart. I ask cardiac patients to remember this point: foods with a rich potassium content are good for the heart—as are nearly all fruits because of potassium values—and foods high in sodium are bad for the heart, as witness table salt.

In addition to heart cases, diabetics ought to be told that blackstrap molasses contains almost no sugar whatever. Since sugar is one of our society's principal causes of heart strain, this is utterly important.

In both the cases of little Gregory and elderly Mrs. Lawrence I used these three great mainstay heart-feeding foods: wheat germ, lecithin flakes, blackstrap molasses. In the lady's case I advised a tablespoonful of liquid lecithin at bedtime in addition to the three spoonfuls of lecithin flakes with the morning cereal, which speeded results enormously.

Bentley was a retired gentleman of 66, formerly tense, nerve strained, many years in competitive banking, now suffering from cardiac hypertrophy—an enlarged heart. This resulted, in my opinion, from overextending in college athletics (on wrestling team), later aggravated by business tensions and insufficient physical activity. One cardiologist had recommended surgery on Bentley's vagus nerve, the chief nerve supply, sometimes named the pneumogastric, to the heart.

The man's face was flushed when he came to me. He suffered frequent headaches. When I took his pulse I found it bounding, jumping, very strong. Questioning elicited that he had an annoying ringing in the ears—all of it confirming that Bentley had what used to be called "an athletic heart," or in common terms, an enlarged heart that took up more than its share of space in the chest. I tested the other major nerve supply just back of his collarbones and these, the phrenic nerves, also bounded and gave signals of palpitation.

Bentley was not stout, but rather trim and neat with a flat abdomen and a well-developed chest that spoke of former athletic prowess. I knew that his vagus nerve should not be cut or in any way disturbed, but what he needed was a very graduated program of exercises, mild at first and working up to where the heart could compensate for its inactivity. Also he needed a succession of very small meals, say, one every two hours.

For all its seeming difficulty this was an easy case, really. The man was happy to have a well-defined, serious program. He got on his back and rode an imaginary bicycle upside-down with increasing speed every day. His frequent (and small) meals were: four tablespoons of wheat germ and a little skim milk in the morning. Two hours later, four ounces of plain yogurt into which he stirred a tablespoon of blackstrap molasses. At the next meal he chewed a dozen raw and unsalted pecan nuts. Then, with each succeeding meal, a small portion of the raw and steamed vegetables listed at the end of this chapter, taken only one kind at a time.

One month later Bentley walked a half mile. In six weeks he went a whole mile at a good clip and his pulse was neither bounding nor irregular. At the end of the second month this seriously sick man was a wholly well man; his heart sounds quite normal and heart size satisfactorily reduced. A suspicious valvular insufficiency had also disappeared. With those amazing healing foods and a health-promoting program, this otherwise problem case responded into health without incidence.

Sylvia was at age 55 a very old woman because of an inflammatory condition of both the muscle tissue of her heart and the lining membrane of the inside heart surface, including the cavities or chambers. When I touched the area over her heart it was very tender—one sign of carditis, as the condition is called. Her pulse was weak and very rapid. When she went to an altitude of about 5,000 feet she suffered grievously, so she could not accompany her family to their mountain retreat. If hurried the least bit, Sylvia just gave out; she could not abide haste in any form. In their commodious home they had to design a downstairs bedroom for the lady of the house, for climbing the staircase was impossible.

Years ago I had learned that in nearly all cardiac cases there was an associated digestive or eliminative problem. (Later I discovered that joining the digestive system and the nervous system resulted in Miracle Health Promoter M, the program that helped

*every case that was at all reversible.) In Sylvia's case, the trouble
was stubborn constipation.*

*Along with the amazing healing foods for the heart listed at the
end of this chapter, I instructed the lady in the use of high-fiber
foods. She had whole wheat germ, lecithin flakes, a mixture of grape
nuts and mouth-sized shredded wheat along with daily leafy vegetables and fresh fruits, all of them supplying roughage for the lady's
sluggish bowels. When I added psyllium seeds during the first few
days of treatment—just a tablespoon of the seeds in eight ounces of
any kind of fruit juice taken twice a day—she began passing copious
stools and this at once took some strain off her heart.*

*I started a careful program of very light exercises along with
the healing foods. In less than two weeks Sylvia reported something
quite strange. "I needed my sewing kit upstairs," she said, "and
went to get it without realizing that I was actually climbing those
long stairs until I got to my old bedroom—something I had not done
in two years."*

*Sylvia's improvement was excitingly rapid. She made it a daily
habit to go upstairs once or twice a day, just for the exercise. She took
long walks in bare feet on her spacious, grassy lawn. By the time she
celebrated her next birthday (her 56th) some two and a half months
later, she was, in her words, "not an old woman but truly young
again." Her husband, Karl, said to me that he and all the family
expected nothing but a decline into death, certainly not this stamp of
renewed health in only ten weeks.*

A "HEALTH INSURANCE" MORNING DRINK

For those who insist on a warm morning drink (and it must
never be truly hot lest it blister the throat lining), then here is a
good habit to get hooked on: plain warm water plus a tablespoonful (or two) of blackstrap molasses and nothing else. This
should be sipped slowly, never guzzled or quaffed like pouring
water down a radiator of one's car. And, as a cautionary note, if
the bowels tend to evacuate black or very dark stools it often
means that the system cannot metabolize all that wonderful
organic iron in the blackstrap molasses, in which case, cut down
the dosage of molasses. If you learn to like this as your morning
drink you will be gifting yourself with true life insurance, so very

good as a life-extender is blackstrap molasses. As I have counseled patients for fifty years, successful heart health comes not
from always doing what you like, but from learning to like what
you have to do. Tie onto this "good habit" of taking a daily
spoonful or two of blackstrap molasses and you will bless the day
you read this book.

Since you already know that wheat germ conveys precious
oxygen to human hearts, here is a delightful way to combine
wheat germ with iron-rich, potassium-rich blackstrap molasses:
merely spread the molasses over wheat germ bread or toast. Easy
to do. Delightful to eat. As healthifying as anyone might want.

It is my firm conviction that if our children were taught in
schools or homes that, instead of destructive bacon and egg
breakfasts, to take on the "good habit" of a morning wheat germ
cereal and wheat germ bread or toast spread with blackstrap
molasses, in one generation the United States would lose its
statistical rank as first in all the world as a country of heart
disease sufferers. Make the kids know that we are also the world's
highest users of white bread, bread from which the wheat germ
has been extracted, and they will grow up knowing how to care
for their cardiovascular systems. With that happy prospect we
can see the end of heart attacks and nitroglycerine tablets in our
future.

Brown rice is another super-important heart-healing food
that I employed in both Greg's and Mrs. Lawrence's cases because of its content of pangamic acid. Pangamic acid is a food
constituent you will want to know about and remember as a
miracle longevity food. It is not only abundant in rice but also in
seeds (both sunflower and pumpkin) and in brewer's yeast.

Shortness of breath that is often associated with cardiac
syndromes frequently responds speedily with the addition of
pangamic-rich foods to the diet. Moreover, when severe heart
pains exist, I have noted improvement in a few days when foods
rich in pangamic acid were used, together with about 600 units
of vitamin E per day. If in addition I employed an ordinary
intake of 25,000 units of vitamin A, say, from fish liver oils,
troublesome heart pains entirely ceased in about two weeks in
stubborn cases.

For children who greatly love desserts, and also for older

persons such as the aforementioned Mrs. Lawrence, I order a daily rice pudding as an after-meal treat. The rice pudding (brown rice only) has a topping of blackstrap molasses and a generous sprinkling of raw pecan nuts, chopped fine or coarse. The nuts are particularly valuable in heart cases because of their content of pyridoxine about which I shall speak directly.

PECANS FOR THE HEART

Pyridoxine has long had its food value to me because of its ability to hasten regeneration of stricken heart cells. It is one of the lesser known factors of the vitamin B family. If the human body that suffers so much mechanically because it functions and labors straight up against gravity's pull, is put back into align-ment so the various parts of the body can perform the jobs for which they were created, the daily ingestion of pangamic-bearing foods helps the heart in a definite manner. It is needed very precisely in the conversion of the amino acids in proteins. Once converted to normal end products of digestion, the con-sumed protein is utilized to replace the damaged cells of the ailing heart.

For best and most effective consumption of pyridoxine, I employ raw pecan nuts. The reader already knows about my enthusiasm for wheat germ and blackstrap molasses; part of this enthusiasm stems from the valuable pyridoxine content within both wheat germ and molasses. If it is referred to as vitamin B-6, that's pyridoxine acid of the B complex.

These pyridoxine-abundant items are healing and life-extending foods in a real sense because of this vital fact: they not only heal but *prevent* heart disease by feeding the nerves that lead to the heart—all this by way of properly converted and utilized amino acids residing in the consumed protein foods. In Chapter 13, Foods That Can Often Regenerate Damaged Nerves, I in-tend to cover pyridoxine more fully.

RICE WATER: THE HEART-HEALTH BEVERAGE

Rice water is the drink I advise cardiac suffers to depend upon. It may be assumed that everyone knows how to make rice pudding or how to cook brown rice; if not, it can be learned quickly by consulting any cookbook. To make rice water, however, one uses four times as much water in the pot as one normally uses to cook plain rice. Allow the rice and water to soak overnight, then cook the rice in the ordinary way. This must be watched because after being softened by overnight soaking, the rice will cook more speedily than one expects. When cooked, what you have is a kind of rice soup. Drain off the rice kernels and save them for a rice dish, keeping a bit of the water for reheating. The rest of the rice water is refrigerated, then sipped as a drink throughout the day.

For those who desire a tasty flavor in their rice water, here again the addition of just a touch of blackstrap molasses provides a delicate cold drink. I advise that it be sipped slowly, never just thrown down the gullet in torrents. And for best results the rice water ought to be used between meals, not at mealtimes because it waters down the stomach enzymes that are prepared to work your foods down to digestive acceptability by the system.

For a warm (never very hot) drink, add a little more than a touch of molasses, even add a bit of lemon juice if desired. Remember, however, not to overdo the molasses. If you used it on rice pudding do not indiscriminately add it to other foods or drinks. The human system cannot use more than a tablespoonful or two daily; if overdone, the resident organic iron will spill over the eliminating threshold and be evacuated as blackish stool matter. Remember that our great-grandmothers gave us sulfur and molasses as the annual spring system cleanser.

WONDERFUL BIOFLAVONOID DRINKS

In all cardiac conditions I have for years advised the generous consumption of bioflavonoids, a substance found in a variety of fresh foods, especially green peppers and oranges, because on the empirical level, bioflavonoid-rich foods speeded recovery of heart disease cases. Not only in colds and infections did I find bioflavonoids a natural healing substance, but in heart conditions bioflavonoid drinks interchanged with rice water provided the best liquid intake I could find.

I sometimes refer to the "bioflavonoid orange juice" as a

desired drink. This means only that the entire orange is cut up and put into a blender, skin and white tissue and seeds and all, then whirled around at high speed to make a delicious natural drink. Within the content of this type of drink is the rich bioflavonoid portion of the vitamin C family that both prevents and treats systemic hemorrhages, rheumatic fever, overly thin and fragile capillaries, even wombs that tend toward miscarriage. In cases of heart disease, the value of daily bioflavonoid drinks cannot be excelled, especially when alternated with pangamic acid-rich rice water.

For the especially valuable type of bioflavonoid drink that I recommend, here is the formula. Prepare the juice of about 12 oranges or the contents of a 12-ounce can of frozen unsweetened orange juice, or, put more easily, a quart of orange juice to which will be added one whole lemon. Cut up the lemon into very small bits, using all of it—peel, white inner sheath, pulp, everything. Pour a cupful of orange juice into a blender together with the finely chopped lemon, whirl at high speed and add it to the rest of the quart of orange juice. Now you have a quart of orange juice plus an entire lemon, and this can be sipped cold or heated to make a quite fine and decidedly helpful morning drink. In my own household I have for years had a warm bioflavonoid drink whenever I desired a heated morning beverage.

MIRACLE SUNFLOWER SEEDS

I have never found an item of desirable protein food for heart patients better than sunflower seeds. I have tried various types of proteins with such cases: cottage cheese, avocado, beans of different kinds (of which only soybeans proved adequate), red salmon, broiled fish (of which halibut and mackerel were best), chicken drumsticks with skin and gristle removed, even many grains. But in the order of their importance and helpfulness in cardiac dysfunctions I established the following. Two ounces of sunflower seeds came first, taken only at one of the several small meals a day for best effect. The other meals are devoted purely to soups, salads, grains, fruits, vegetables, etc. Next in importance came egg yolks, but only in heart cases, for reasons which I shall give presently. Next came pumpkin seeds, only two ounces at a meal, raw (untoasted) and unsalted and hulls removed. This is especially recommended in heart cases of males with prostate gland problems. Wheat germ eaten as a protein would come next. Then soybeans, broiled fish, red salmon, cottage cheese, chicken legs.

It is important to take no more than about two ounces of hulled sunflower seeds and make a meal of it with a raw vegetable salad. For dressing on the salad I strongly advise a teaspoonful or two of wheat germ oil, for the oil contains that vitamin E factor that enables one to "make do" with the poor quality of air in our polluted atmosphere. It is also urged upon heart cases not to eat protein items at other meals than the one where sunflower seeds is the main item.

Protein is absolutely vital to the health of any human being. But the human system cannot store it as it can fats or starches (which pile up as extra weight and make you fat). However, while vital to human existence, the body's capacity for metabolizing protein is sharply limited to no more than two ounces a day at the very outside. This is acutely evidenced in cardiac cases, for they respond sensitively to protein intake, good or bad. When good, as in the use of sunflower seeds, recovery is hastened. When bad, as with red meats or preserved fishes, cheeses, delicatessen products, their protein overload putrefies into three smelly acids—indol, skatol and phenol—which gives human stool its characteristically bad odor, and this slows recovery to a halt. Those with chewing problems or false teeth may purchase an inexpensive nut grinder at a health food store for under twenty dollars and grind the sunflower seeds (or pumpkin seeds) to a fine and manageable consistency.

Now the matter of eating eggs ought to be considered forthrightly and scientifically. In almost all cases I am against the use of eggs, most especially the eating of egg yolks, for they do indeed raise the blood cholesterol level. Yet in heart cases I actually advise the consumption of as much as one egg a day, preferably poached or medium boiled, never soft-cooked or raw.

Does this represent an inconsistency? Why should I strike out against eating eggs in general and advise the taking of an egg a day in cases of cardiac dysfunction? The reason, stated succinctly and scientifically, is this. The ailing heart needs choline. Choline is a substance found in good quantity and quality in egg yolks. British journals of research have documented this fact beyond reasonable doubt. Therefore, despite its other negative factors, I do advise a limited use of eggs in heart cases.

What about the cholesterol business? Recent pontifications of governmental Health Advisory Boards refute the old idea that eggs should be avoided because they tend to raise our cholesterol level in the blood. Since the body itself manufactures cholesterol, say these "authorities," it does not matter how many eggs one eats or doesn't eat. To such a declaration I say piffle and balderdash. These men with impressive authoritative titles cannot know anything about sick people on the pragmatic level when they say that in their "studied opinion" diet really doesn't have anything to do with health. "Merely eat a balanced diet with something of each food classification," they say, "and that is all anyone can do about health, diet-wise." I consider such an opinion unworthy of serious consideration. If these "authorities" ever had to deal with actual cases of sick human beings they would know that any person, *without exception,* with a high cholesterol count increases the count when consuming a couple of eggs as a daily breakfast item of nutrition. Contrary to this, when a person actually sick from overly cholesterol-rich blood reduces or eliminates the use of eggs the cholesterol level goes down and down and down.

It is true that one's liver makes cholesterol even if we do not overeat cholesterol-bearing foods. But what we cannot control we just cannot control. It is what we can control that concerns us. Surely we can control the manufacture of cholesterol *in addition* to what the liver produces, and this is done through eliminating eggs and other cholesterol-abundant foods.

Yet—despite all this—I actually advise heart patients to consume one egg a day. It is exactly because the choline that is needed by the damaged heart is so abundant in egg yolks that in this instance the advantage more than compensates for the disadvantage of egg consumption.

In all cardiac cases I most strongly recommend the taking of a good quality of vitamin E, those usually available in health food stores rather than those manufactured by pharmaceutical firms. In most cases I have found 600 International Units to give good results, say 200 I.U.s after the morning, noontime and evening meals. Because vitamin E is an oil-soluble substance, it is better to take the 200 units after meals—preferably after meals that have some oil content (such as salad oil on raw vegetable salads) than before meals.

A good way to ensure the consumption of vitamin E is to take a teaspoonful of wheat germ oil daily in heart cases. I advise taking this at bedtime, when it interferes with no food in the stomach and is most readily absorbed and utilized. Taking a daily teaspoonful of wheat germ oil is a pleasant and safe way to buy life insurance, adding years to life and life to your years.

MORE WHEAT GERM WONDERS

Here we come to the food item that is most nearly the miracle longevity food with respect to vitamin E and the heart. It is wheat germ. It is the same food we covered in detail in the beginning of this chapter. Consider the following, please.

Two research workers of Milano, Italy, Magno and Rovesti, came up with a most significant finding in the field of wheat nutrition. By extracting the juice as it comes from the field they found that this wheat juice from whole wheat had special benefits for the victims of heart disease. Not only that, but the same juice pressed from whole wheat markedly helped prostatitis in the male, painful menstruation in the female, even impotency of a progressive nature. On boring into the reasons for all this helpfulness it was learned that these healthifying results stemmed from the high quality of vitamin E in the newly extracted wheat germ juice. It helped establish the presently accepted fact that a very high quality of essential vitamin E materially benefits the heart as well as the reproductive organs.

This much, then, about primary foods for the heart.

In considering garlic I am myself not exactly sure whether its classification should be primary or secondary in dealing with heart-healing nutrition. Garlic is so good and useful an item in cardiovascular cases that it almost belongs up there with wheat and blackstrap molasses and lecithin and the rest.

GARLIC: NATURE'S OWN ANTIBIOTIC

Raw garlic is a classic longevity food of especial value in cardiac disturbances. Most people already know about the usefulness of garlic in reducing hypertension. People with abnormally high blood pressure have used garlic here and abroad in such large numbers as to establish its clear value beyond any peradventure of doubt. And the *oil* of garlic has been known to still the terribly frightening pain of angina pectoris in a mere five days.

If you or a loved one suffers angina pain I suggest you try this miracle longevity food, but only in the raw state and in large doses. I recommend several cloves of finely chopped garlic swallowed down with distilled water, say, two or three times daily, chiefly between meals.

It should interest all of us that the work with garlic done by the Soviets has caused the item to be labeled "Russian penicillin." This label has validity. It is the best natural anti-infection food item known to man. Within the system, it acts with almost the pharmacological power of penicillin or the other antibiotics, but without side effects. By swallowing chopped raw garlic as aforementioned, there is no offensive breath. After continued treatment of oneself with raw garlic, however, there is some exudate or emanation of a slight garlic odor from the lungs, but this is so low-grade as to be inoffensive.

We all know that heart attack victims are rushed into oxygen tents on arrival at hospitals. We should in this context also know two factors: one, that garlic abates and often wholly eliminates the agonies of angina; two, that a single spoonful of wheat germ oil daily provides about as much oxygen to the stricken heart as can be provided by a conventional oxygen tent. The reader will hopefully note the value of combining these two miracle longevity foods in heart problems. Since I established the policy in cardiac cases of daily doses of both wheat germ oil and raw garlic, all patients with heart problems got well better and faster *naturally*.

Another point of importance here. Even when garlic is not taken by mouth but merely crushed and the vapors inhaled, it appears to help. For years I have advised the vapors of garlic instead of old-time smelling salts when one had "the vapors," as they used to be called.

One final word. Because it became known as "nature's own natural antibiotic" by reason of its detoxifying and anti-infection qualities, I and other doctors in the forefront of nutritional advances have used raw garlic as a paste applied to open wounds with incredible success. Even when flesh is gouged from the body and we have an open gaping wound, garlic paste applied directly into the wound *prevented septicemia* (blood poisoning) in cases where septicemia was an expected sequel. And although some nutritionists have called garlic an intestinal irritant, I do not agree; and even if it were, the value of raw garlic for heart problems and for a variety of other ailments clearly outweighs any possible demerits.

Let us consider yogurt as a kind of secondary or "helper" miracle longevity food for the heart. In all cases I refer to plain yogurt, never the kind that is fancied up with sweet fruit jellies that I consider abominations. If indeed one needs fresh yogurt sweetened, a dollop of honey will do the job.

There is an importance to yogurt aside from its value to heart patients and those with digestive difficulties. I speak of fungus infections. Yogurt, in common with buttermilk, and also to a great extent sour milk, contains an abundance of lactic acid bacilli. These microorganisms protect you against the fungi which seek to successfully invade your innards. If you have ever had a case of athlete's foot you know how well-nigh ineradicable are these fungus infections. But if you have a good, high-grade implant of lactic acid bacilli they will hold the fungi in check and you are not likely to suffer any fungus misery.

All readers who have ever taken a course of antibiotic drugs for any complaint at all should have been told that antibiotics tend to destroy these marvelously protective lactic acid micro-organisms. That's why we so often see rectal itching and cracked corners of the mouth; it's the fungi having a field day in the body and working into orifices because the antibiotics have killed the lactic acid bacilli that normally hold them in check. Therefore, without fail, I advise the taking of at least one 4-ounce cup of yogurt, and even two such portions, every day until you have reimplanted a new intestinal flora. This you will know when the itching ceases and the tongue or mouth heals.

To some extent the sulfa drugs also kill the lactic acid bacilli. Now the reader can realize the importance of a work like this where natural, health-giving miracle longevity foods are given for various illnesses, rather than drugs which have side effects and can destroy the inner protective organisms.

If your doctor who prescribed the antibiotics did not tell you to take yogurt (or buttermilk) following his course of treatment, I can say frankly out of years of experience with drug-prescribing doctors that either he did not know that his antibiotics destroyed bodily protective microorganisms in the fungi class and the lactic acid bacilli needed to be restored, or he did not care or was too busy to take the time to free you of future ailments.

To tie all this together, to prevent suffering all kinds of infections after antibiotics because you lack the "good" bacilli to protect you, you are advised to consume every day from four to eight ounces of yogurt, or a full quart of buttermilk from skimmed unpasteurized milk, or bulgaricus or acidophilus milk. This must be continued every day for about one month. It will reimplant the needed intestinal flora and provide protection against internal infections.

For double value in heart cases as well as digestive ills, flavor your cup of yogurt with a full tablespoonful of blackstrap molasses. If really keen about gaining natural health rapidly, I also advise sprinkling a dash of chopped pecan nuts on top for a sundae-like effect.

In my own home as a special treat I make the following dish. Spoon the yogurt out of the cup into a dish. Pour a tablespoon of blackstrap molasses over it. Sprinkle a good handful of finely (or coarsely) chopped raw pecans on top of everything. Then, as the big prize, add wheat germ in plentiful supply to everything and you have something better than anything the United States Pharmacopeia can offer.

Although not strictly classifiable as a food, I take the liberty of including brewer's yeast as a healing food item for the heart. In another context, yeast is a good source also of nerve food, and when you are nerve-strained or are given to nervous crying jags, a spoonful of yeast powder in a glass of distilled water or together with spoonfuls of plain yogurt, will often steady you remarkably and quickly. In this context, however, the daily use of debittered yeast is strongly urged because it contains biotin for the heart. Biotin is another of those natural specifics for heart pain. It has no side effects whatsoever. If the yeast makes one gassy, then a bit of lemon in the water with which it is swallowed tends to hold down gas formation.

NATURE'S BEST DIURETIC

And now we come to a mountainously important diuretic in the area of natural foods which also serve as miracle longevity foods. I refer to watermelon. It is not only a valuable heart food, but one of the most effective food items for ridding the water-logged body of excess fluids.

But here, sticking to my treatment of heart cases, I emphasize the use of watermelon as a mealtime drink. A drink at one's meals? Yes, precisely so—and a good one. Here is how to use it.

Since I am against taking beverages at meals because they water down the enzymes that have to work on the consumed foods, and thinning down the strength of enzymes results in poorer digestion, I have to supply a substitute for those who feel they absolutely must have a drink to swallow or wash down their every bite of food. For such persons I advise a small slab of watermelon cut up into tiny mouthfuls. When the food is chewed down and ready to be swallowed, do the swallowing along with a small cube of watermelon. Since the fruit is preponderantly water anyway, you will be consuming the finest water available. Unlike tap water with its chlorine, fluorides, and other chemicals and pollutants, the liquid in watermelon has been purified in nature's own laboratory, warmed by the sun, refined within its bed of pulp, filtered into purity through the roots and branches of the feeder lines. Nowhere on this globe can anyone have a finer, purer, safer drink than that in watermelon. I advise parents to acquaint their children with this. Make them become slaves to this good habit, a habit that enslaves as well as any bad habit ever did.

Remembering that watermelon should be consumed in small bites (equivalent to sipping rather than guzzling water), it can be made into small balls or cubes and brighten up desserts or used as decorations around other dishes. Some use watermelon balls on top of yogurt. Some remove the seeds and then cut the pulp out of the cold watermelon and swirl it around in a blender to make a cold picnic drink of delicious natural flavor. If you like, add a portion of rice water and give it another whirl to make a bubbly rice-and-watermelon champagne swirl. Add a melon ball to all this and you have a kind of cocktail.

A final secondary heart-healing food is plain whole wheat toast when spread with blackstrap molasses. I advise this for children to add good heart health to their growing years. I advise this also for adults who do not feel up to their day's chores unless they have toast of some kind and a cup of beverage. In such cases whole wheat toast spread with about one tablespoonful of blackstrap molasses, plus a warm bioflavonoid drink, plus a bowl of wheat germ, lecithin flakes, skim milk, and fresh fruit, provides such solid healthifying nutrition that—I hesitate to say this—even if one violates the rest of the day, he or she will have laid in enough to keep health going.

PREPARING AND COMBINING HEART-HEALING FOODS

The following are several suggested ways to use the aforementioned heart-healing foods, all of which were used in the schedule of restoring health to little Gregory with his troubling rheumatic heart and elderly Mrs. Lawrence with her aggravated cardiac arrhythmia. Instead of leaving a sufferer of any kind of heart disease in mid-air wondering exactly what to eat and what to leave alone, these and all other heart patients were given the list of the heart-helping foods mentioned above, and also a list of what follows so that they might know how to combine and prepare them for taste and palatability. In most cases, what they enjoyed most was my not ordering exactly when to use which miracle longevity heart food, but to use them all in a variety of combinations throughout the day, as their tastes dictated.

Wheat Germ—is used as a morning cereal, used in a soup if desired, used frequently to sprinkle over soups and salads and whatever else suited them. The idea was to take into the system a good supply of raw wheat germ, always tested for rancidity by smelling before using.

Lecithin—used in the form of lecithin flakes, is available in all health food stores and in many supermarkets. Use about three or more tablespoons of the flakes as an addition to wheat germ cereal, or add to soup and salads. If you are sufficiently Spartan to take it in liquid form, which is by far the best way, I usually advise taking it at bedtime for greatest benefits, swallowed down with a bit of distilled water or herb tea or swallowed down with plain yogurt. If you doubt the value of this lecithin treatment, just have a blood test for cholesterol levels before starting and about two months after the daily lecithin intake.

Blackstrap Molasses—used in a morning cereal is a most palatable way that agrees with almost everyone. About one level tablespoonful is advised. If you use more, watch the stool evacuations to note if they turn black, in which case the system tells you it cannot absorb and utilize that much of the blackstrap molasses. The wonderfully strengthening organic iron in the liquid is more than the body can use; in short, cut down to one tablespoonful or even less.

Do not let any store that does not stock blackstrap molasses convince you that other brands of molasses are just as good. Insist on the blackstrap variety, with that distinctive burnt nut flavor. If you put a banana into a blender and whirl it until it is a creamy substance resembling ice cream, you can top it with blackstrap molasses and make it a delicious dessert, even adding chopped pecan nuts, always the raw kind, to make it even better and more heart-healing a food. I have advised using the molasses over rice pudding (whole brown rice) and patients have reported that it is an enticing addition. Diabetic patients in particular should become acquainted with the uses and riches of blackstrap molasses.

Brown Rice—may be used as a dessert in the form of rice pudding, or as a main starchy meal as a soup. Two cups of water to one cup rice usually does it fine, but one should follow the instructions on the package because each company has evolved its own best way of preparing the rice. When you add blackstrap molasses to the rice pudding, as mentioned above, you add additional health benefits to this item of nutrition.

In some heart cases also plagued with digestive problems I advise the brown rice as a complete meal, all by itself, as the entire noonday lunch, with only a fruit breakfast (cherries, grapes, persimmons, peaches, raw peeled apples, nectarines—as much as you want of any one of these) and one protein item as the evening meal chosen from among these: sunflower seeds, two ounces of pecan nuts raw and unsalted, a small portion of broiled mackerel or halibut. Choose any of these together with a raw vegetable salad (which is neutral and combines with anything). If you follow this, the salad should have plain yogurt only as dressing. If oil must be used, only wheat germ oil, one level teaspoonful, is advised.

Pecans—must be taken raw for the best heart-healing effect and they can be taken as a two-ounce meal all alone, or in chopped form, sprinkled over salads, soups, and desserts. An effectively beneficial sundae is made by using a dish of plain yogurt to which is added a tablespoonful of blackstrap molasses, then a generous sprinkling of both pecans and raw wheat germ. The pyridoxine content in pecan nuts that helps regenerate damaged hearts can best be appropriated by the human system in two-ounce quantities, and can be overdone, so no one in my opinion should eat immoderate amounts of raw pecans in the manner of consuming popcorn. What benefits reside in pecans are applicable also to nervous patients because it is pyridoxine that supplies specific food for the nerves, as will be discussed later in this book, so a daily two-ounce portion of raw unsalted pecan nuts is recommended for both heart and nerve-problem cases.

Rice Water—is a quite satisfactory drink provided one does not quaff it at mealtimes. I recommend that you take the last rice water drink about a half hour before a meal and then not again until about two hours after a meal, always sipping the drink slowly. In my view, a quart or more of rice water should be kept in a refrigerator by every cardiac victim.

Bioflavonoid Drinks—are useful in most cases of heart disease as a liquid refreshment, but in cardiac cases where arthritis is an additional problem, the use of citrus juice is usually best avoided. But this is not always true; you must try it for yourself. Some heart patients do well with bioflavonoid drinks even if they have arthritis or rheumatism. Actually, bioflavonoids can be procured from eating green peppers in generous quantity in raw salads, and in such cases I advise the addition of a teaspoonful of wheat germ oil as a salad dressing. In some cases I have advised making a bioflavonoid drink merely by putting green peppers and spinach plus lettuce into a blender or juicer, thus bypassing citrus fruits altogether.

Sunflower Seeds—taken in about two-ounce proportions make about the best protein meal I have ever encountered in the treatment of cardiac cases. They should be hulled, washed before use, then either chewed and well masticated or, in cases of elderly folk with dentures, ground fine and masticated thoroughly. With serious heart distress, when the patient is ready to take protein nutrition, I advise sunflower seeds and a raw salad topped with wheat germ oil as a dressing as the entire meal. A replacement for sunflower seeds is pumpkin seeds, especially for men with maladies of the prostate gland. When the heart patient has additional problems with digestive capability, what often helps greatly is grinding down the sunflower seeds to a fine talcum powder consistency and mixing this with yogurt as an evening meal all by itself. If people with insomnia are awakened and unable to return to sleep, sometimes this combination of sunflower seeds and yogurt will raise the blood sugar level sufficiently to get them back to sleep.

Eggs—may be poached or boiled, not fried and never soft-boiled or taken raw. British researchers have observed evidence that raw eggs tend to make a coating on the human intestinal lining. Like mineral oil that also coats the intestinal mucosa, this prevents the absorption of nutrients, sometimes to the extent that people who consume quite nutritious foodstuffs at the same time almost starve to death. The egg yolks, wherein is contained the choline that benefits the damaged heart, should not be altered or adulterated by the addition of table salt—not even herb salt—or other spices.

Vitamin E—is often unbelievably beneficial for heart patients. Cardiac victims find it difficult to handle the polluted air we must breathe. It is the carbon monoxide in the air that distresses them. When they do the diaphragmatic exercise that I prescribe (raising the arms and panting like a dog while the midriff goes in and out to exercise and strengthen the diaphragmatic breathing muscle), especially just before retiring, and also take 200 International Units of vitamin E after meals, they can handle or "make do" with the atmospheric pollutants. It should be understood that the heart of the cardiac patient usually does not receive all the blood it needs for its own operations by way of the coronary arteries, which are often clogged or occluded. So here is where vitamin E comes in. It enables the heart to function fairly well with some 40 percent less blood. (To cap the victory over heart distress, add about two thousand milligrams, or two grams, of vitamin C to the daily diet.)

Vitamin E is important enough in heart cases, I feel, to set down and even repeat what it does within the organism.

1. It dilates the arteries, thus helping the entire circulatory system.
2. It prevents coagulation or the formation of clots, which block the passage of blood in the arteries to the heart—the very clots which often bring on heart attacks and kill.
3. It preserves the oxygen content within the blood and enables one to carry on with what blood one has, reducing the need for more.

(*Note:* Each of the aforementioned primary heart-healing foods, and also the secondary heart-helping foods that follow, are at the same time also healing articles of nutrition in another category or two, having recognized health merits for other conditions besides their usefulness for the heart. Accordingly, many of them that have been fully discussed above will not be repeated in detail where they are recommended for other than heart ailments. Example: blackstrap molasses as a miracle longevity food for the brain. Under Chapter 2, Eight Available Foods That Add Power to the Brain, the reader will be referred to this chapter for a full coverage on blackstrap molasses.)

Garlic—is a secondary food that in some ways is also a primary heart-healing item of nutrition. I refer always to raw garlic, although the cooked variety is also a welcome addition to soups and vegetable stews. I advise garlic in sandwiches and in soups and of course, in garlic bread. To add spice and healthful-ness to an otherwise unexciting item, make quick garlic bread by spreading on plain whole wheat toast a mixture of wheat germ oil and mashed garlic, seasoned lightly with powdered kelp. Some savants and political leaders in India attribute their longev-ity and clearmindedness to taking a clove of raw chopped garlic as often as four times a day.

In heart cases I often have had dependably good results by recommending one or two finely chopped cloves or toes of garlic taken before breakfast each day, swallowed with a little rice water or bioflavonoid drink. If you suffer the extreme pains of angina and happen to own a garlic press, try using the extract or oil of garlic in small doses for about five days and running and note the difference in your well-being. And if you are prone to infec-tions or feel that your "inner plumbing" is toxic, frequent doses of raw garlic is a way to detoxify your system that is as good as anything I know short of a 3-day fast followed by two weeks on a mono-diet. This will so quickly change the body chemistry and detoxify a body laden with accumulated, uneliminated debris, that you will graphically understand why garlic has been called "nature's own natural antibiotic."

Yogurt—is especially desirable and healthifying after a course of antibiotic or sulfa drugs because such drugs tend to kill the protective lactic acid bacilli in the system. If one does not care for plain unsweetened yogurt, sour milk or acidophilus or bul-garicus milk will do as substitutes. In many cases I have advised patients merely to let a quart of whole milk stand in the sun for a day or two, thus making homemade sour milk of the finest quality with a very high content of the desirable protective bacilli. To reimplant the needed new intestinal flora, I recom-mend taking the yogurt or sour milk in the morning before breakfast, or between meals when it need not mix with other food intake, or the last thing at bedtime at least three hours after the evening meal. The program should be continued for about a month.

Another useful and beneficial way to employ yogurt is to take it when you awake during the night and are unable to return to sleep. A small dish of plain yogurt with half a banana sliced into it will quickly raise the blood sugar level and help the insomniac get back to sleep.

Yeast—or any product of the B vitamin family is useful nutrition for the nerves, especially for those who get tense in advance of giving speeches, dinner parties, etc. Adding a teaspoonful of powdered, debittered brewer's yeast to a daily cereal is a good way to consume the needed daily protection afforded by vitamin B. For children, it can be stirred into fruit juice and lost or disguised that way; for adults, it may be taken in tablet form. Taking yeast for vitamin B content is to be preferred over liver because a full third of the animal blood is at all times in the liver, and if the beast is sick in any way some of the sickness will be in the blood of the liver that is eaten. Because of its biotin content, yeast is a daily *desirable,* a miracle longevity food not to be overlooked in cases of distressing heart pains.

Watermelon—is an especially beneficial "drink-food" in heart cases because cardiac victims are so often in need of a diuretic, being waterlogged or prone to holding too much fluid in their bodies. Drug diuretics forever have the disadvantage of side effects that heart patients can well do without. But a full day or two on only watermelon, with a small cube of the fruit popped into the mouth all day long at about five-minute intervals, will unload the system of fluids that you will think you have never taken on board in your entire life. Also, if you just cannot eat without some drink with which to wash down each mouthful, have at the side of your plate a small slice of watermelon in place of the usual glass of water or beverage, and take a tiny bit of the fruit to serve as a drink.

While water or a common beverage will dilute the strength of stomach enzymes which await the processing of your meal, watermelon fluid is at least quite entirely pure, unmixed with chlorine or other chemicals, and to a great extent, a real food instead of an inert, unneeded slosh of water that only thins down and reduces the quality of the digestive enzymes.

Whole Wheat Bread—or whole grain bread is a useful heart-healing food to a limited degree because of the d-alpha tocopherol content that, hopefully, is not entirely lost in the baking or toasting process. Plain or toasted, whole wheat or whole grain bread can be made more useful for those who feel they must have some kind of bread with a meal by getting into the habit of using blackstrap molasses as a spread in place of butter or margarine. Sometimes the addition of lecithin flakes or raw wheat germ on top of the molasses makes an appetizing, and certainly more healthifying slice of toast. If bread is not required, however, I advise brown rice as a starchy food if one does not feel thoroughly fed without some starchy item at mealtimes.

SUMMARY—HEALING FOOD LIST FOR THE HEART

Principal heart food: WHEAT GERM

Assisting heart foods: LECITHIN
BLACKSTRAP MOLASSES
BROWN RICE
PECANS
RICE WATER
BIOFLAVONOID DRINKS
SUNFLOWER SEEDS
EGG YOLKS
VITAMIN E
GARLIC
YOGURT
YEAST
WATERMELON
WHOLE WHEAT TOAST

2

Eight Available Foods That Add Power to the Brain

If you are interested in developing better and stronger brain power you must remember the word *lecithin*. It may be the key word in all the remaining days and years of your life.

Just about one-fifth of your brain is composed of lecithin. This wonder-working substance that is obtained principally from soybeans is also a constituent of every cell of your body. It is in the makeup of all your bone cells, your muscle cells, your gland cells and skin cells and everything else besides your brain tissue. From reading Chapter 1, Foods That Build Up the Heart, you already know how important a healing part lecithin plays in heart disease. This is so because lecithin is needed by damaged heart cells to restore the sick organ.

But here I wish to concentrate on the brain. I must tell you the story of Saul, the bookkeeper. He was a middle-aged man, almost always tired and a bit fat, who dimly felt he was capable of better things if only he knew how to go about it. In a dentist's office he had picked up a magazine with an article that recommended lecithin as an acceptable healthifying food in place of the riff-raff junk foods that people customarily stuff into their stomachs. Then he happened to run into the product and decided to try it.

Let me tell you Saul's story almost verbatim as I recall it.

"Here I was, 42 years old and still just a bookkeeper, just a cog in the big wheel of my company. Every night I came home tired, yawning, no steam in me for even playing such simple mental games as Monopoly." As he spoke these words he appeared contemplative, groping inwardly with a sad, self-pitying expression on his face.

"My brain felt foggy," he continued, "as though there was dust or something in my skull. Besides everything else," he said, his hands patting his abdomen, "I was carrying too much gut.

"Then I read this short article about lecithin. By chance I went into a health food store for some raw milk and spotted a metal container of liquid lecithin on the shelf right in front of my nose. I recalled the article and on impulse decided to buy the stuff and try it. That was it. I took a tablespoonful morning and night and in two weeks I wanted to do something after work— something like an evening course in accounting, which I did. I lapped it up. Did well. Even had energy left over for learning to play bridge." He paused, looking at me questioningly. "How could just one food do all that magic in a single month?"

At the telling of all this, Saul was about to take his CPA exams. Already he was earning well, was happy with his life, had even trimmed down some of his protuberant belly. He had come to me for a bothersome hip lesion but told me about his experience with lecithin because it was a member of my profession who had written the lecithin article that changed his life.

I told Saul about the eight amazing healing foods that had the remarkable virtue of adding power to the brain. Besides soybeans, I said, the nation's population would do well to know about such other lecithin-rich foods as those three valuable seeds: sunflower seeds, pumpkin seeds and sesame seeds; then also raw pecan nuts, raw garlic, raw wheat germ, brown rice and, as a drink, the rice water in which it is cooked.

While treating Saul for his hip problem I counseled him to do the following things.

"I am going to instruct you to do the Primordial Walk and a few other self-aligning body movements. The Basket Roll and the Sway-and-Arch will enable your body to more thoroughly utilize the lecithin in all these foods. Such vital movements that align the body are what may be called the Miracle Health Promoter M. Then, since you are already so far along in your knowledge of how lecithin helps unfog the brain, I am going to show you how to go much further along this road by consuming about a dozen raw unsalted pecans every day, a clove or two of raw garlic daily, any or all of those three seeds (sunflower, pumpkin, sesame) as your dinner protein, say, four times a week, raw wheat germ as your daily morning cereal, a dish of brown rice as your principal starch item for a while, and the rice water in which you've cooked the rice as a cooled-down drink whenever you desire a beverage."

Saul followed this faithfully, glad to have a definite program instead of the hit-and-miss way he was consuming lecithin. Of his own accord he repeated to me, as an exercise in memory, the following wonderful words:

> *Soybeans, the three seeds (sunflower, pumpkin, sesame), raw pecans, raw wheat germ, raw garlic, brown rice—these are the eight amazing healing foods that are rich in lecithin and add power to the human brain.*

I advised him to add such "helper" foods as bioflavonoids, which will be discussed later, and watermelon and vitamin E, and in two months' time he was so exuberantly well as to make to me a statement that I feel should be ineradicably inscribed in the marble halls of our departments of education, as follows.

"If we could get the young people of our land into the habit of consuming every day some or all of these eight lecithin-rich foods, by the next generation I firmly believe we would have a people of mental giants instead of the enfeebled crop of present-day vandals and muggers and dope users."

RINSE AWAY SLUDGE IN ARTERIES TO THE BRAIN

The amazing healing foods that are rich in lecithin, plus the employment of the Miracle Health Promoter M, worked similar wonders in the case of the headachy, fuzzy-brained mother of four who had not been helped by conventional treatments of any kind.

Eileen said later that she would never have thought her

continuous, grinding headaches and confused mental state could be cleared in six weeks. She had had the condition since early girlhood and was now in her early forties. It had been so bad that she couldn't make it through her first year in college, was not able to concentrate enough to study, had no possibility of passing her term exams. But a mere month on the following schedule rid Eileen of headaches altogether, then another two weeks swept every fog and cloud from her brain, seemingly. Here was the eating schedule that made Eileen a well woman, plus the daily alignment movements that constituted the Miracle Health Promoter M.

THE BRAIN FOOD PROGRAM

Morning (upon rising): One tablespoonful liquid lecithin along with 1,000 milligrams (one gram) of vitamin C. In combination with vitamin C, lecithin tends to rinse away the sludge in arteries and unclog them so that circulation to the brain becomes unimpeded.

Breakfast (one hour later): A fruit breakfast consisting of watermelon in any desired quantity, up to a half pound of seedless grapes, all the peaches or papaya she could eat.

10 A.M. (midway between breakfast and lunch): An 8-ounce glass of freshly squeezed carrot juice, or apple juice, or just plain rice water (water in which brown rice has been cooked).

Lunch: Large plate of green leafy salad vegetables plus tomatoes, raw zucchini squash, radishes, onions, raw mushrooms if available. Add liberal sprinkling of powdered kelp and a tablespoonful of wheat germ oil. Use plain yogurt as dressing if topping is desired. One cooked (lightly steamed) vegetable such as eggplant to supply intestinal fiber, or carrots, cauliflower, broccoli, kale. Add several cloves of garlic when steaming the vegetable.

Midway between lunch and dinner: One or two cloves raw garlic, finely chopped, taken with either carrot juice, watermelon juice, apple juice or distilled water. Take one tablespoonful of blackstrap molasses after taking the garlic and beverage.

Dinner: Two ounces of either sunflower seeds, sesame seeds or, especially if lacking in sex drive, pumpkin seeds, finely ground if chewing is difficult. A small cereal dish of whole wheat germ, lecithin flakes, skim milk and any added raw fruit desired (bananas, peeled apples, peaches, pears). No drinks permitted. Use sips of skim milk if you must have a beverage to swallow mouthfuls of food.

Bedtime: One tablespoonful liquid lecithin plus 1,000 milligrams of vitamin C.

After a short time on this quite powerful anti-brain-clogging program, along with the physical drills in the Miracle Health Promoter M routine, Eileen came up with rather astonishing remarks.

"I feel alert in my head," she said, grinning happily. "I'm clearheaded for the first time, would you believe it? I even want to do crossword puzzles. And now I am playing Scrabble, my head's that well screwed on now." She spoke about the eating program adding power to her brain. "Now I really know for sure," she said, "that I need a lot of lecithin in my system to clear my thinking and prevent a blocked blood circulation to my brain. Would anyone believe that just six weeks ago I was not able to think worth a fig!"

Eileen knew the value of soybeans, but their steady use became a bore. I then instructed her in an interesting new way to capture their goodness and benefits.

SOYBEAN-AND-GARLIC TOAST

"Do you like toasted bread?" I inquired. When she said she did I told her to make whole wheat toast and use soybeans as a spread in place of the usual butter.

"Chop up a lot of raw garlic," I said, "or mash it down finely. Add it to cooked soybeans that you've also mashed down to a buttery fineness, then use the mixed soybeans and garlic as a spread on the toast." It was easy. Since she was a great bread eater she was anxious to begin. In short order she consumed in a very pleasant way both the desired lecithin, by way of soybeans, and the raw garlic. Later, as a further departure from boredom,

I added blackstrap molasses to her drinks as the preferred sweetening agent (to provide a lot of organic iron for her energy), generous helpings of both raw and boiled onions, frequent servings of two ounces of sunflower or pumpkin or sesame seeds as her protein dish and about 800 units of vitamin E after meals.

We both discovered that her best lunch was a large green leafy salad and a dozen raw pecan nuts, for she did well on this, reporting steadily improved circulation to her brain area by way of accelerated mental ability.

"Truly," she said earnestly, "these foods plus the Miracle Health Promoter M give me added brain power. I play Scrabble like a champion now," she laughed. "I'm developing a powerful brain to reckon with."

UNRETARDING "RETARDED" FRANCES IN TWO MONTHS

It's odd how people with below-average brain power seem to know each other. After Eileen was pronounced well and discharged, she came into the office with a friend, Frances, who, it developed, had been joining her every morning in the movements that replaced their bodies in structural alignment and were designated Miracle Health Promoter M.

Here is what the 52-year-old Frances told me.

"Ever since I've been doing the same exercises and things with Eileen I've been feeling better and getting more strength and stuff out of my meals. They sometimes say I'm retarded but it isn't true; I'm just dull in my head and have been since an automobile accident 20 years ago. It's made me slow down and I have to talk real slowly to collect my thoughts. But I am not retarded, I'm sure I'm not."

Upon further inquiry I learned that both ladies had their morning fun and benefits from doing three things together. One was to lie on their backs and ride a bicycle upside-down. The other was to run races on hands and knees up and down the long basement playroom of Eileen's home, finishing by a lot of sway-and-arch movements of their spines. The third was the all-round Primordial Walk that appeared to help and strengthen every muscle, tendon, cartilage and ligament of their bodies. What this did was place their bodies in mechanical alignment and enable their digestive organs to better assimilate the values out of the foods they consumed—an authentic "miracle health promoter" that came to be known as Miracle Health Promoter M.

"I feel so much better doing all this with Eileen," said Frances, "that my family says I ought to come to you for the whole program."

In Frances's case I at once added to the physical routine a lot of daily walking with the instruction that she count four while inhaling and tick off her steps to the count of six while exhaling. This aided the respiratory function by supplying more oxygenated blood to her brain. As she exhaled to a long count, she was forced to tighten and strengthen the diaphragm, the chief breathing muscle of her body, and as this diaphragmatic breathing showed results, I advised her to extend the walking count to six while inhaling and to ten or even twelve as she exhaled.

When Frances started on her list of foods rich in lecithin, her system absorbed its brain-healing magic like a dry sponge absorbs water.

One day about a month later, her brother, who was two years older came in for a talk and to extend enthusiastic congratulations. "We've been unfair to Francie," he said, "because we really acted as if she was retarded when it was certain she wasn't. How could she have been when now in just a month she talks just as chipper as almost anyone? It must have been a mistake, making such a diagnosis. She wasn't anything like retarded before that big whiplash accident in the car years ago."

The man had unknowingly hit upon a salient truth. In my long professional experience I had seen others after an accident had strained the mechanical parts of their bodies out of kilter, like a car that drags to one side because of distorted center of gravity after a collision, and this prevented their system from utilizing the nutrients in the foods they consumed.

Frances memorized the eight readily available foods that add power to the brain, and used them with unabating diligence. She soaked soybeans overnight regularly and then cooked them over a low, slow heat, after which she mashed them into a paste the consistency of butter, adding chopped garlic for further enrichment and spicier taste. As a morning cereal she took without fail, a dish of raw wheat germ to which she added at least two tablespoonsful of lecithin flakes, topping it with one table-spoon of blackstrap molasses. "I like it," she said. "It tastes like nuts and I'll have this for breakfast all my life."

With growing mental alertness and awareness the hereto-fore "retarded" lady became inventive. Gaining much daily energy from blackstrap molasses she devised a beverage of rich value, namely, heated skim milk into which she stirred a table-spoonful of molasses and both bone meal powder and brewer's yeast.

"It makes me sleep sounder," she said, which was indeed true when taken at bedtime.

She boiled brown rice to use as the chief starchy food almost daily, taking the rice water as a supplementary drink. For snack-ing while watching television, she ate raw pecans while others in the family consumed potato chips and soft drinks laden with refined sugar. As a mainstay protein, her choice was sunflower seeds, occasionally changing to lightly broiled mackerel or halibut, both of which I could recommend in the fish depart-ment, sprinkling the fish liberally with powdered kelp.

All this, in slightly under two months from the day she first entered the office, made Frances a normally bright, energetic and happy person who looked back on her slow, dull-witted, misnamed "retarded" past as an unhappy dream.

Four months later, or six months after she began the health-building, brain-feeding program, I heard from her younger sister that Frances had enrolled in a night education class so she could "learn to read and write better," having missed (or lost, or forgotten) some of her skills during the years of mental dullness. Later she even began to compose little pieces for the piano, for she'd been born with a musical ear and this came forth demandingly after her recovery.

SUMMARY—LIST OF FOODS THAT ADD POWER TO THE BRAIN

Principal food: LECITHIN (liquid and flakes)

Assisting foods: SESAME SEEDS
                     SUNFLOWER SEEDS
                     PUMPKIN SEEDS

                    BLACKSTRAP MOLASSES
                    PECAN NUTS (raw, unsalted)
                    WHEAT GERM
                    BROWN RICE

Secondary helpers: GARLIC (raw)
                    VITAMIN C
                    VITAMIN E
                    RICE WATER
                    BIOFLAVONOID DRINKS (see Chapter 1)
                    EGGPLANT
                    RAW ONIONS
                    BOILED ONIONS
                    WATERMELON
                    ASPARAGUS (canned)
                    RED SALMON (canned)
                    MACKEREL (broiled)
                    HALIBUT (broiled)
                    KELP
                    ALL FRESH FRUIT EXCEPT SOUR PLUMS
                    ALL FRESH VEGETABLES EXCEPT
                    RHUBARB

3

Five Ordinary Foods That Strengthen the Lungs and Bronchial Tubes

A magnificent food that hardly gets mentioned but deserves to be known by all sick people with afflictions of the lungs or bronchial tubes is cranberries.

It is a food that I have found beyond doubt healthifies the human lungs and bronchial tubes, and thus is a godsend for asthmatics, those with emphysema and similar ailments. Also, because cranberries are so valuable for the entire breathing apparatus they should be known and frequently used by those with cold hands and feet and other circulatory problems.

The research into cranberries began nearly 50 years ago when I was new in practice. A policeman with severe asthma had gone down to 95 pounds. He labored so strongly for each breath that he could eat nothing, had no desire for any kind of food. His solicitous family always tried to tempt him with goodies but he would take hardly anything. Then, while in hospital over the Thanksgiving holidays a sympathetic nurse brought in a tray of turkey and cranberry sauce together with the other usual trimmings. She coaxed him to eat something—anything—so he reluctantly reached for the cranberries. Surprisingly, he ate it with relish.

"Could I have some more of this?" he asked. She hastened to bring him another, and then one more. From that day he began to improve. And this triggered my research into cranberries and what there was about them that dilated the human bronchi and enabled people with asthma to breathe.

By a happy research concatenation, the quest for cranberry values led to other foods that helped strengthen the lungs and bronchial tubes, making it unnecessary to shoot into the bloodstream of asthma sufferers injectibles such as adrenalin with their widespread, imponderable side effects. In addition to cranberries I found that miracle longevity foods for respiratory ailments were wheat germ, brown rice, yeast and kelp. Since memory is fickle but paper never forgets, I ask the reader to write these foods on a handy card or notepaper. Even besides these five extraordinary foods for the lungs and bronchi there are other secondary, but also very great, foods for respiratory conditions, namely, lecithin, garlic, sunflower seeds and vitamin E. But the greatest of these is cranberries.

WHEAT GERM AND OTHER WONDER-FOODS

A single teaspoonful of wheat germ oil can at times convey as much oxygen to the heart, and then around to the body, as an oxygen tent, so wheat germ and wheat germ oil are great discoveries for your breathing organs. Lecithin can clear away the clogging debris (cholesterol, etc.) that prevents a free flow of oxygenated blood all round the body, and oxygen is the breath of life, you know. When the body lacks in vitamin E there are often cold extremities, such as feet and fingers, due to the same insufficiency of oxygen flow to the parts. You can see the interconnecting factors in all this, can't you, and why a list of enormously valuable miracle foods such as the above ought to be kept handy and memorized for daily use?

Some other pointers, while we are at it. For reasons not yet clearly understood we think more clearly with a high garlic intake. And thinking requires an oxygen flow to the brain. In many brain disorders or disturbances there is a noticeable lack of vitamin E. The same lack of oxygen that produces heart attacks and slow brain activity can be the true culprit behind asthma, shortness of breath, other breathing difficulties, and even some ailments as seemingly far removed as skin lesions.

The surface in food research has barely been dented. I myself have conducted 102 independent research projects not under the thumb or misdirection of self-serving medical or pharmaceutical interests, and even after these 50 research years there is a mountain of work yet to be done to shift us away from drugs into miracle foods for various human ailments.

The policeman, a large-framed, raw-boned, first genera-tion Pole who'd sunk to 95 pounds, filled out his skeleton-like body with enough weight to rejoin the police force—and what did it was the use of miracle foods, plus a few body-aligning exercises (which I refer to as Miracle Health Promoter M) to enable his system to utilize the food values. The foods were those on the previously mentioned list. The exercises were crawling on hands and knees, then racing on hands and knees; raising his arms and panting like a dog to exercise the diaphragm, which is the chief breathing muscle; clasping his palms behind him at the waist and rolling the elbows inward to straighten the spine and enlarge the chest capacity; and most of all, doing the Primordial Walk—all of which are further described throughout this vol-ume.

STILLING THE TERRORS OF ASTHMA

An elderly automobile painter had almost as much asthmat-ic trouble as the policeman, and he also came back to normality by following a program of these foods and exercises that re-turned the malpositioned vertebrae of the spine into proper adjustment.

When Elmer entered the office I could hear far back in my consulting room at the rear of a long hall, his labored breathing and musical chest in the front waiting room. At times his fellow workers had to bring him into the office cradled in their arms like a baby, so labored was his breathing and so great was his misery. In Elmer's case the true "open sesame" to health was a combination of cranberries and lecithin, both of which I wish to discuss here.

Cranberries contain a mysterious something that acts in the manner of the bronchial antispasmodic that medical people employ (such as adrenalin) to dilate the bronchial tubes. During an attack, because the bronchi contract and do not allow the contained breath to get out (although the sufferer thinks he cannot catch his breath when in fact he can't get rid of the one he's got), a bronchial antispasmodic drug such as adrenalin injected into the bloodstream works on the controlling vaso-dilator nerves and forces the bronchial tubes to open, thus permitting breathing to ensue. In the same way, technically, cranberries serve as vasodilators. They tend to open the con-tracted bronchials and enable regular breathing to proceed.

Fresh cranberries are of course preferred, but even the canned variety often does the work satisfactorily. I dislike the preservatives and sweeteners that go into canned cranberries but what appears to help the asthmatic is the antispasmodic ingre-dient in the berries, so it works even when adulterated with inimical additives.

When cranberries are in season I advise buying several pounds, which can be prepared and stored by refrigeration. To prepare, fill a cooking pot halfway with cranberries and add water to the top. Then simmer over low heat until the water evaporates down to the level of the berries. The water is then run out and the berries are mashed through a strainer so that the skins are held back and the pulp of the fruit is collected in a jar. You refrigerate this jar of cranberry pulp and use it when needed.

When the asthma sufferer gasps for breath, a spoonful or two, large or small according to taste, in a cup of warm water usually suffices to give relief. The pulp is merely stirred in the water, then sipped slowly. After two or three sips the victim's bronchial tubes usually open and normal breathing begins. To see this healing food do its magic is to be genuinely thrilled.

If cranberries are too tart for one's taste, they may be sweetened with blackstrap molasses or honey, as one wishes. In all cases of asthma history I recommend that cranberry sauce be the preferred dessert; use it regularly at least once a day.

Along with frequent daily dishes of cranberry sauce, Elmer was also ordered to take three daily tablespoonsful of liquid lecithin along with lecithin flakes in his morning cereal. Why all this lecithin? Well, here's why.

Lecithin is highly rich in organic phosphorus. From earliest times phosphorus has been known as "brain food." The reason for this is that slow-brained and witless persons customarily do not have a sufficient blood circulation to the brain, while taking phosphorus-rich foods stimulates a flow of oxygen-laden blood to the brain. Additionally, and please read Chapter 1 for more on this, the power of lecithin to rinse away and cleanse the arteries of clots, clumps, and piled up sludge interfering with the flow of blood around the body, is almost phenomenal. In my cases of elderly people with memory lapses, lecithin intake caused almost all of them to enjoy renewed mental alertness and memorizing prowess.

RAW GARLIC HASTENS RECOVERY

When garlic is also employed, as with Elmer who consumed several cloves of chopped raw garlic every day, the results are both speeded and magnified.

Now that the reader knows this about miraculous cranberries and lecithin and the other nutrients, he can appreciate the words of Dr. Harvey W. Wiley, original founder of what became the Pure Food and Drug Administration, when he declared: "In the future our foods will be our medicines and our medicines will be our foods."

In addition to cranberries and lecithin and garlic, Elmer became enthusiastic about the other foods that were recommended. Although a painter of little schooling, the man was a born philosopher. As he began breathing "as though I belonged to mankind," as he put it, he said it did not matter whether or not he liked any food because—note this—:"If it's good for me I will learn to like it." That was the attitude with which he took to eating a wheat germ breakfast, brown rice every other day for lunch, a tablespoon of brewer's yeast and a teaspoon of kelp at bedtime drunk down with distilled water, 800 units of vitamin E (200 after each meal and 200 before retiring), and a large handful (about two ounces) of sunflower seeds along with his daily raw salad plate.

EXERCISES FOR ASTHMATICS

For his daily exercise routine I advised the following, which I would recommend to others with asthmatic or emphysematous ailments:

1. Primordial Walk
2. Dowager's Hump (hands behind back and roll elbows inward)
3. Diaphragm Drill (hands above head and pant like a dog)
4. Basket Roll (lie on the floor on the back with knees drawn up to chest, hands clasped and body tightened into a little basket, then roll from side to side)
5. Knee-Chest Rest (rest several times daily on knees and elbows crosswise on bed with head hanging slightly below level of the bed)
6. Walking to In-Out Count (take long walks and count to four while inhaling, but count to six while exhaling, thus exercising and strengthening diaphragm to improve breathing)

On almost similar programs of these miracle foods for the lungs and bronchial tubes, plus a few mild exercises to self-adjust the body into mechanical alignment, within six months the policeman said, "I thought each day was my last and now I'm back on the force as a working cop," and Elmer, a man in his 60s, said, "I thought every day was the last one and now in only three months I feel that I've got 20 good years ahead of me."

The magic inherent in these programs is not only for the few, for similar near-miracles happened to Mrs. Kay, a lady in her late 50s and a longtime sufferer from bronchiectasis.

Mrs. Kay was finicky about foods and her slim, gaunt body showed it. She hated cranberries and declared she would have none of it except, maybe, some cranberry juice as a drink, but this I forbade because it's the pulp in the berries and not the juice that does the job for the bronchial tubes. She did however like soybeans, which helped mightily because I could get lecithin into her weak body by way of mashed soybeans thickly spread on whole wheat or wheat germ bread.

AN AMAZING BRONCHIECTASIS CURE

Because both bronchial tubes were enlarged and constantly filling with pus in the lady, my problem was how to stop the formation of mucus in her system besides getting nutrition into her to build some weight on her bones. First of all I stopped the intake of all mucus-forming foods: eggs, salt, cream, hard cheeses, butter, meat fats, oils, lard, preserved or smoked meats and fish in the delicatessen line, sugar and white flour products—all bakery goods. Then, in addition to the five miracle foods for the bronchial tubes and the other secondary helper foods, I concentrated on such mucus solvents as all kinds of berries (fresh strawberries, blackberries, etc.), oranges, grapefruits, lemons, limes. For long rest periods every day Mrs. Kay was ordered to lie crosswise on the bed with her head hanging over the edge of the bed lower than her body, as though hunting for shoes under the bed; also to rest betimes in the knee-chest position with head over the edge of the bed. All this was to achieve upside-down drainage of the bronchial fluids.

In a surprisingly short time we encountered a miracle. After just a week of eating large amounts of wheat germ toast spread with mashed soybeans plus frequent cups of warm water flavored with alfalfa tablets, for I had ordered no fewer than 16 alfalfa tablets a day for her, she almost entirely stopped spitting up the frothy green fluid that was filled with pus cells. The lady had given up hope and was wearily resigned to her fate; but now she gained a spark of enthusiasm, so it was my time to have her do what she'd earlier refused to do.

"You must take cranberries several times a day," I ordered. She was willing, although she made a wry face in agreeing. "And here is a program to make you fill out that skinny body," I added, and to this she willingly assented. It happened that when she saw the program she was almost ecstatic about it. Here is what brought the miracle to pass, along with a few simple exercises to make these miracle foods assimilable.

FOUR MIRACLE DRINKS

First, a choice of four drinks: Alfalfa tea, water with black-strap molasses, bioflavonoid drink either cool or warm, or rice water. If possible she was to rotate and have all of them from time to time.

Second, her solid foods, which included the miracle cranberries, wheat germ, brown rice, sunflower seeds and kelp, besides the secondary helpers such as large daily doses of raw garlic, liquid lecithin, lecithin flakes in her wheat germ cereal, vitamins E and C every day, contained the following special items to make her gain weight healthily and properly: sun-dried dates as a between-meals snack, a whole avocado at lunch daily (because of its natural and assimilable fat content), and about a half dozen ripe olives every day, which the lady dearly loved.

In less than one month this longtime bronchiectasis sufferer ceased spitting and hawking altogether. "I haven't been without a cough since a seige of bronchitis many years ago that started this bronchiectasis," she said gratefully. Her chest felt different, she said, and examination by a chest specialist confirmed that both bronchi that were enlarged and always filling with pus were now of normal size and quiescent.

As her increased weight warranted, I asked Mrs. Kay to push herself with more Miracle Health Promoter M exercises, for as she gave up energy in the movements I recommended, her body generated new and more energy, which is a central principle of exercise. That is, when you expend strength in proper exercises the body rejuvenates you with more returned power, but if you rest entirely you lose what little energy you had.

BODY-ADJUSTING EXERCISES

The added exercises for this lady, and for others who wish to gain and maintain health in this unhealthy world, were as follows:

1. Basket Roll—described elsewhere in this book.

2. Squat Walk—which merely means getting into a low squat and walking around the room until vaguely tired.

3. Head Lift—which consists of trying to lift the head off the shoulders, meanwhile turning the head in both directions, thus tractioning the parts and relieving existing nerve pressures in cervical vertebrae.

Mrs. Kay was five feet seven inches in height and weighed 102 pounds when we began. Two months later she not only lost a serious ailment that had plagued her for 20-odd years, but gained a steady three pounds a week to a weight of 122 pounds.

Her eyes sparkled as she bade me goodbye when I discharged her. "What wonders God hath wrought," she quoted with feeling. "To think of the years and thousands of dollars I wasted because I knew nothing about these miracle life-giving foods!"

SUMMARY—LIST OF FOODS THAT STRENGTHEN THE LUNGS AND BRONCHIAL TUBES

Principal food: CRANBERRIES

Assisting Foods: WHEAT GERM
BROWN RICE
YEAST
KELP
SUNFLOWER SEEDS

Secondary helpers: GARLIC
LECITHIN (liquid and flakes)
VITAMIN E
VITAMIN C
ALFALFA
AVOCADO
RIPE PURPLE OLIVES
RICE WATER
BIOFLAVONOID DRINK
BLACKSTRAP MOLASSES

4

Miracle Nutritional Aids for Digestive Disorders

The most common digestive disorder I have encountered over the years was plain, uncomplicated constipation, a complaint easy to correct in almost every case that had not depended on laxatives for years and years. Next in frequency, I think, was hemorrhoidal problems, largely as a result of straining at stool because of constipation, sometimes from sitting on cold seats for a long time, sometimes also from sitting over long periods in any one position, as in truck driving—always, I have discovered, the end result of two things: insufficient bulk or fiber in the diet and pressures on nerves leading to the digestive organs which prevent the flow of power to these organs.

In addition to constipation and piles, a common digestive ailment is sour stomach or too much acid and belching, burping, flatulence associated with cramping or pain anywhere along the alimentary canal.

Such a case was Sally, a maiden lady of some 40 to 50 years (she would not tell even me her exact age), who was a supervisor in the telephone company and had suffered for years from constipation. She had a case of bad breath that was noticeable even from a distance when I stood talking to her. Inquiry revealed that she usually took a hurried breakfast of scrambled eggs, white toast and black coffee—nothing else; then a toasted or barbecued sandwich and Coca-Cola for lunch; later a "good dinner," as she called it, of a chop or two, plus cooked vegetables and stewed fruit, eaten while she read the newspaper or curled up with a book. She had barely any fresh fruit, no exercise worth mentioning, a raw salad plate only on rare occasions, fresh air during her walks of a few blocks to and from the bus that took her to her work.

Straightening out Sally's constipation and halitosis of some years' standing was easy, really. She began her days with a bio-flavonoid breakfast that consisted of liberal quantities of oranges and lemons—the entire fruit, along with the yellowish skin or tissue between sections of the oranges and lemons that contained rutin, that wonder-working factor also known as vitamin P. Along with this she learned to eat a dish of grains, either brown rice with its valuable pangamic acid or wheat germ with its host of health-giving values (see Chapter 1).

Since she lived alone and could perform what would be awkward or foolish looking in public, she began doing the squat exercise both before breakfast and just before retiring. This merely consisted of squatting down as far as she could and walking or waddling around the room until her thighs and pelvis were tired. It was a means of elongating the rectum and colon while stimulating the parts into activity. Within two weeks this alone started bowel evacuations and reduced the bad odor in her breath.

At about the same time as this I was seeing George, a carpenter who forever chewed gum in the belief that it sweetened the breath as the advertising misguidedly declared, and suffered great pains because of a rather severe case of diverticulitis. At that time the prevailing medical "authoritative" opinion was to avoid coarse raw vegetables in diverticulitis, but I'd especially encouraged huge raw salad plates at least once a day in such cases, and George was half-frightened when I ordered this in his diet, although now the "authorities" say they have come to realize that raw fruits and vegetables are useful items in diverticulitis.

George was nearly 60 and had endured rather stubborn piles along with his intestinal diverticulitis and constipation problems since he was thirty. I learned that his custom was to sit eating his lunch on cold stone steps; thereafter, oddly he thought, the hemorrhoids always seemed to flare up. When I explained that it would be better to sit eating his lunch and also dinner at home on a warm or mildly hot water bottle in order to let the rectal and anal tissues absorb the heat emanations for the duration of the meal, he did this and improved at once.

The gum-chewing habit needed to be dealt with. I did so as I gave him a list of my research findings for cases of constipation—the same list that helped Sally overcome her problem in short order.

First, then, about chewing gum. The ads say that it aids digestion but I have found beyond doubt that it *un*-aids digestion in quite a specific way for a specific physiological reason. Here is why.

CHEWING GUM UN-AIDS DIGESTION

Gum chewing requires constant swallowing. As one swallows the saliva, what is also swallowed is a digestive enzyme in the saliva that's needed in the first step of digesting starchy foods. By continuous swallowing of this enzyme, ptyalin, the glands that produce it are overworked, really exhausted. You have used up the enzyme for no reason at all, with no starches to work on. Then when you do eat bread or rice or other starchy foods, your exhausted salivary glands cannot secrete enough ptyalin and the food is swallowed unworked upon, or not sufficiently digested in the mouth as it should be. It therefore lies in the stomach fermenting and souring because it has missed the first step in starch digestion. Any wonder the breath becomes foul and belching or burping ensues?

When this was explained to the carpenter he made a face of disgust for the doctors who hadn't told him this and stopped chewing gum as firmly as he'd quit sitting on cold stones and aggravating his hemorrhoids.

Both George and Sally considered the list I gave them to be of great value, and rightly so, for it was their guide to pain-free longevity. Since in my experience there are more digestive complaints among most people, young and old, than any other except possibly the complaints about rheumatic and arthritic pains, the following Guide List ought to be required reading in our schools during the growing up years of our children so that they may become healthy adults.

After a kind of preamble declaring that in our society so many food items are so adulterated and denatured that there is ample reason for digestive upsets, the Guide set down the program, which in my studied opinion would help almost all classes of stomach and intestinal problems to a rather great extent.

GUIDE LIST FOR GOOD DIGESTION

1. Do not water down or liquefy meals and your enzymes by thinning them down with drinks at mealtimes. Let your enzymes employ themselves full strength on your foods, not watered down. If you absolutely think you cannot do without washing down each mouthful, use small cubes of watermelon for this purpose.

2. Eat small meals. Eat often if necessary, but always only a little at a time.

3. Between meals, rest on knees and elbows (the knee-chest position) and while thus positioned suck your rectal parts inward and then let them out, doing this several times to exercise the pubococcygeal muscles that also strengthen the sexual function and at the same time improve peristaltic activity for better bowel movements.

4. Eat mostly fruit if possible, and chiefly raw foods at any one sitting whenever this can be accomplished. Human beings started as fruitarians. Fruit is their natural food, and when in trouble, eat only fruits for about a week and note what happens to your state of health as you give yourself this physiological and digestive rest during which your system can sort out its problems and repair them. The body is self-healing and it knows what's the matter even when your doctor doesn't.

5. Don't swallow any biteful of food until it is well chewed and liquefied in the mouth. Swallow each individual bite *before* you reach for another. Learn to put down

your fork while chewing, between this mouthful and the next. This alone has saved doctor bills and harrowing pains for many persons with digestive ills.

6. Do not let yourself be talked into drinking milk because it is "a good protein," or because "no one ever outgrows his need for milk." Your body just isn't set up to cope with protein that is drunk rather than chewed. Your body is not a car radiator; don't dump fluids down your gullet, especially protein fluids, which the enzymes cannot handle coming at them in a torrent.

7. When over-proteinized, as I have found most sick persons to be (not under-proteinized as the propaganda has it), eat only raw nuts, either whole or ground, such as pecans, almonds or cashews, or seeds such as sunflower, pumpkin or sesame, as your entire protein intake for a week. This enables the organism to balance its protein metabolism, and its requirements. It can do no harm, but only good, if followed for a single week.

8. When you have consumed too much protein, and your body tells you after Thanksgiving or Christmas dinners that you have overeaten turkey or other meats, take a teaspoonful of apple cider vinegar after the meal, or an equal amount of dilute hydrochloric acid, especially if you are an older person, to assure the needed HCl for digestion.

9. If you must have hot beverages, make them warm instead of hot; and make them either a mixture of water and blackstrap molasses, or alfalfa tea, or warm bioflavonoid, or heated rice water, rather than coffee or tea or cocoa. Also—very important—sip the drink, never guzzle it.

10. Take no drugs whatsoever, unless absolutely driven to them (that's so rare as to be almost impossible), for even the allegedly mild ones such as aspirin have possible side effects and cause diseases which pyramid in your body. Pyramid—how's that? Well, the first drug results in some side effects (and hardly any drug in the pharmacopeia is entirely without some side effects), then

you take drugs for the side effects problems, and these second drugs cause in turn new side effects for which you take other drugs that cause other side effects—ad infinitum. It is my studied opinion that the drug-taking route is the road to an abbreviated longevity.

11. If you have a diarrhea problem take raw apples for their pectin value, especially on retiring. Other foods with healing value for diarrhea that I have researched are persimmons and raw tomatoes.

12. Along with other foods for constipation I can recommend figs that have been sun dried, never artifically dried in sulfur baths. It appears that the tiny seeds in figs gather mucus and intestinal debris as they are conveyed along by peristalsis, washing out of the system large residues of theretofore uneliminated waste products.

13. As a between-time drink, I have never found anything quite as effective as cabbage juice, sipped slowly and not quaffed like pouring water into a funnel. Cabbage is easily liquefied in a common blender. Another drink that is a natural laxative (especially in pancreatic cases, as will be seen in Chapter 6, Incredible Miracle Longevity Foods for the Pancreas), is made of warm water spiced with blackstrap molasses.

14. Vying with papaya, which is not always procurable, the one great food for digestive ills is plain yogurt. It may well be called a wonder food, so helpful is it in virtually all digestive ailments and so protective is it in nearly everyone's life.

The great Russian scientist, Metchnikoff, proved beyond any doubt that yogurt (or sour milk, clabber, acidophilus milk or any milk product in which bulgaricus or lactic acid bacilli are present in high abundance) tends toward gifting the consumer with longevity way into the century mark. Over many years of practice I had one catchall technique for digestive maladies when all else failed or when I was baffled: "Four ounces of plain yogurt first thing in the morning and the same the last thing at night. Sweeten it with blackstrap molasses at least one of those two times. In the morning, wait at least an hour after the yogurt and then eat a cereal bowl of wheat germ mixed with more yogurt and fresh fruit in season."

AVOID COFFEE AND COMPANY

While urging yogurt on digestive patients I also prohibited the use of coffee because it tends to cause a biotin deficiency. Elsewhere, in the chapter dealing with miracle foods for the heart, you have read that biotin is naturally and exceedingly valuable for heart pains. If the patient had been taking barbiturates I strictly forbade this, because barbiturate drugs, in common with cigarette smoking, destroys the body's vitamin C that the system needs as its chief anti-infection safeguard. In addition, all foods with sugar in them and all baked goods with starch in them were not permitted until further notice—a notice that was never given. During this period of good miracle foods, and no destructive foods, the digestive organs and also the heart had a chance to self-repair and assure an extended life expectancy.

At no time are people with digestive ills allowed to take mineral oil as a laxative because this destroys practically all vitamins such as E, A and D that are oil-soluble. Figs and blackstrap molasses and alfalfa tea are miles ahead of any oil laxative.

Alcohol also destroys vitamins, so it is off limits for persons with digestive problems. I believe that doctors who advise small nips of alcohol "to sharpen up appetite" ought to reread their physiology texts and not floor patients with such nonsense.

When papaya is available, by all means consume it as a protein digestant, especially after a meal where protein foods are eaten. Curiously, the papaya that is slightly unripe is richer in papain, the protein enzyme, than the thoroughly ripe papaya that has already undergone what I call *sugarization*.

THE BEST PROTEIN FOOD

When in doubt as to which out of many kinds of protein to choose, ordinarily you will not go wrong if you select sunflower seeds. No more than three ounces of this, and two ounces are enough for most people. Eat this at noon, then take no protein items at all with the other two meals, confining yourself to fruits, vegetables, cereals, soups, salads, starches. (For the miracle that sunflower seeds can work in cases of visual ailments see the text in Chapter 14, Seven Foods That Often Renew and Revive Visual Health.)

A final word about yogurt. People with digestive upsets are often poor sleepers. We know that organic calcium promotes sleep. Yogurt is rich in calcium. It is even richer when sweetened with blackstrap molasses, which also offers an abundant calcium supply. At bedtime, therefore, it makes good sense and good digestive chemistry to spoon out a few spoonfuls of yogurt blended with blackstrap molasses; then be prepared for "nature's sweet restorative" (as the Bard called sleep) to take peaceful possession of you. In similar context, if awakened and unable to return to sleep, this yogurt-and-molasses combination is likely to beat a sleeping pill in effectiveness—and absolutely no side effects.

Sally had a photocopy machine in her office and she generously made copies of the above Guide List for friendly "fellow sufferers," as she called them, under her supervision.

She was forbidden to read while eating; for this robs blood from the digestive organs, where it is needed, to the brain where one must interpret what is read. And she was prohibited to take enemas, a habit she'd gotten into for her constipation. "The human rectum and colon are self-cleansing," I told her, which surprised her. "They were not intended to be artificially washed, with possible fluid balance upsets, any more than human nostrils were made to be sprayed or eyes were made to be doused with drops."

In eight weeks she was entirely well. "I'm joyously free of constipation," was what she told me with gratitude and enthusiasm. What did it and also forever (one hoped) took away her bad breath, was following the Guide List above, plus the list of foods given in the Summary at the end of this chapter, meanwhile doing the walking and squatting exercises and the knee-chest resting periods.

"I truly, deliciously feel like a new woman. . . who would

have thought it!" she declared when I let her go at the end of eight weeks.

George also, in about ten weeks, was discharged and decidedly happy about his renewed health. He appeared a bit worried about his diverticula, however, so I explained matters to him.

"Everyone has diverticulosis to some degree, George," I said. "It is only when those pouched-out, little sausage-like extensions ballooning out from the intestines become inflamed that you add "itis," which means inflammation, that becomes diverticulitis. But if you follow this list, or even *almost* follow it, you are never likely to have those pouches fill with rubbish and set up an inflammatory state."

The Guide List became George's "Bible." I called him two years later to do some carpentry on my porch deck and he was healthier, more spry and happy, than he'd been for a long time.

"It's been ten years or more, maybe twenty, since I've been and felt this good, Dr. Morrison," he said with conviction. "Eating these miracle foods is a joy, feeling so good is more joy, and the exercises you gave me keep my spine in such good adjustment that I hardly ever need to go see a chiropractor anymore."

SUMMARY— LIST OF MIRACLE FOODS FOR DIGESTIVE DISORDERS

Principal food: YOGURT (or clabber, sour milk, acidophilus)

Principal food No. 2: PAPAYA (whenever available)

Assisting foods: FIGS
PERSIMMONS
SUNFLOWER SEEDS
PECANS
RAW APPLES
BLACKSTRAP MOLASSES
CABBAGE JUICE
WHEAT GERM
RAW TOMATOES

ALMONDS
APPLE CIDER VINEGAR (or HCl tablets)
ALFALFA TEA
RICE WATER DRINK
BIOFLAVONOID DRINK
WATER AND MOLASSES DRINK

5

A Fine Food Foursome That Rejuvenates the Liver

The principal healing food that often produces near miracle results in liver ailments is, in my studied opinion, BREWER'S YEAST.

It deserves to be set in capital letters, as above. I also consider, and have often written, that tomatoes constitute a precious food for the liver that may be considered a kind of "food-medicine," and this is true. But more recent studies have convinced me that first and foremost, even topping tomatoes in value for enlivening and rejuvenating the liver, is plain, debittered brewer's yeast. It is a food item that is not only a medicine but a virtual miracle that lengthens life.

HANDLING THE ALCOHOLIC

A thin, wasted, middle-aged alcoholic named Roberto, from a distinguished Spanish family, proved quickly and graphically the value of brewer's yeast, especially when taken in abundant quantity at the same time as eating tomatoes at almost every meal. His condition had been diagnosed as cirrhosis of the liver, a sad and serious label to hang on anyone. He expected no results.

But recover he did—and quickly. Three times a day he fairly stuffed himself with tomatoes, all kinds of tomatoes, raw, boiled, stewed, baked. Before breakfast he had a glass of un-salted tomato juice with a spoonful of powdered brewer's yeast. At noon the yeast was sprinkled on his salad. At dinnertime it was stirred into his tomato soup. And what this accomplished in unbelievably fast time was a renewed portal circulation that had clogged his liver; a regeneration, thought impossible, of de-generative cells in his liver; a replacement of fatty infiltration by healthy liver tissue.

For too many years Roberto had been drinking alcohol while not eating enough or often enough. Now he was set on the following course of rejuvenating his wasted body with miracle foods eaten with frequency, plus exercises to reoxygenate and realign his mechanically maladjusted spinal structure and bodily frame.

Instead of alcohol, barley water became his daily drink. His salads were laden with fresh raw radishes, both red and white, even black radishes when available. In place of bread or other grains, his regular starchy food for energy and muscle strength was dried brown rice. Sunflower seeds and pumpkin seeds were his mainstay protein items. Lecithin flakes were poured into his wheat germ cereal and more lecithin in liquid form was poured into his stomach, a full tablespoonful morning and night. It was fortunate that raspberries were obtainable and that he liked them as a daily dessert. His program was entirely angled toward a miracle recovery—a test of the workability of miracle foods—and he came though the test with almost perfect health in a matter of three months, gaining thirty pounds meanwhile, going from 115 to 145 pounds.

"I am here but I do not believe it," said Roberto three months after he began the rejuvenating miracle program. "I am well and really strong and am what you may call an effective human being today, but only three months ago I thought my family was hiring the gravediggers to send me back to my ances-tors."

RECOVERY FROM LIVER DAMAGE
PLUS LEAD POISONING

Nearly as great a miracle was the recovery of Spencer, a retired linotype operator who was almost 70 years old and had a clear-cut case of lead poisoning besides a very sluggish liver. He was heavy with creases of tissue that looked like biscuit dough, attributed his weariness, his sluggish liver, his lack of desire for any activity, to being too fat. But an examination showed otherwise.

He said that a lot of times various foods tasted like metal. He also had occasional nausea and stomach cramps. This caused me to look into his mouth and there it was: the blue line at the gums that was pathognomonic of lead poisoning. His many years at the linotype machine had caused him to inhale enough lead to produce the trouble.

Among other things, Spencer suffered from impaired nutrition that needed to be handled radically. There were impediments to the flow of blood through his liver—what is called portal hypertension, something like high blood pressure in this great big organ, the liver.

WHY LIVER IS A TWO-WAY STREET

Now let us learn a simple but essential lesson in human physiology. At all times one-third of your blood is in your liver; the liver is not really an organ but a gland, the largest in the body. Because it harbors so much of your blood at all times, and I think the same is true in animals, I do not allow anemic patients to eat liver unless they know personally how the animal was raised and know that it was not sick before slaughter. As the Bible puts it, "the life is in the blood," and with a third of bodily blood in the liver, whatever sickness was in the animal at slaughter time can be transmitted to the person eating its liver. Therefore, while liver can be good nutrition, it can also transfer much sickness.

In Spencer's case it was necessary to go at his impaired nutrition first of all by washing the excrescences out of his stomach. I put him on only watermelon for a full day, eating a small cube of the fruit about every five minutes and opening up his urinary function like a hydrant in operation. Last thing at night I had him eat a couple of ripe Bartlett pears, which further acted as a diuretic and had him urinating all night. The disturbed sleep was justified. (By the way, I have had similar cases, and almost as bad, in women who used leaded cosmetics and acquired lead poisoning; in such cases, after initiating treatment,

I taught them that beauty is the result of what you put *into* the body rather than what you put *on* the body.)

As in Roberto's case, the miracle food foursome I gave Spencer was brewer's yeast and tomatoes plus radishes and lecithin. The yeast gave him the needed B vitamins for the loss of functioning liver cells. The tomatoes—ah, there was a kind of authentic miracle for liver cases because tomatoes appear to contain a substance that is something like the medical man's quinine and I have satisfied myself many times that, even in severe hepatitis cases (one recently in my own family), tomatoes and hardly anything besides tomatoes for a day or two puts into metabolic gear immensely desirable changes. If the companion food becomes brewer's yeast, then the liver cases that I used to find so very hard to handle became, in most instances, quite satisfactorily remediable.

Because there is always a vitamin E deficiency in liver cases, in my observation, I advised 800 units of vitamin E daily for Spencer in addition to the liquid lecithin with its valuable vitamin E content that he took first thing in the morning and last thing at night. Besides this, his only allowable cereal became wheat germ with its own vitamin E values.

His daily salads were piled high with tomatoes and radishes. Daily tomato soups were liberally sprinkled with brewer's yeast powder. He liked to go out on the exercise field for the self-aligning exercises I gave him, and he took along yeast tablets to swallow with his thirst-quenching tomato juice that he carried with him in a thermos jug. To thin him down at the same time, his Miracle Health Promoter M exercises were as follows:

EXERCISES TO ADJUST YOUR OWN SPINE

1. *The Basket Roll.* Lie on back with knees drawn up to the chest and hands clasped to hug yourself tightly into a small basket. Roll from side to side, first slowly and then rapidly, to exercise the lateral ligaments of the spine and work the malpositioned vertebrae, if any, back into alignment.

2. *Breathing In-and-Out Count.* Walk on grass with bare feet

and count to four while inhaling, then to six while exhaling; later to six and eight, etc. As the exhaling count is lengthened, the diaphragm tightens and the breathing apparatus is strengthened.

3. *Race on Hands and Knees.* This also should best be done with bare feet, on early morning wet, dew-filled grass where possible.

4. *Sway and Arch.* Get on hands and knees and dip spine down, then arch it up as high as possible. Do this to low back area and to area between the shoulder blades.

5. *Squat Walk.* Squat down as far as you can (in the manner of defecating before toilets came into use), and in this position walk, or waddle, around the room or back yard. Do this especially upon rising.

6. *Diaphragmatic Breathing.* Raise arms to open chest cage and with lips slightly parted pant like a dog, noting how the flesh at your midriff (the diaphragm) goes in and out during the panting. This diaphragm strengthening and reoxygenating drill is best done just before retiring. What you gain at bedtime you retain during bedtime.

7. *Primordial Walk.* Walk on hands and feet rather than on hands and knees. This enlivens and strengthens every muscle, tendon, ligament and cartilage in the body.

8. *Upside-Down Bike Ride.* Lie on your back and raise legs, then pretend you are riding a bicycle upside down, forward and reverse.

9. *Dowager's Hump.* Clasp hands behind you at level of your waist and roll elbows inward, which lifts chest and straightens spine.

Within two weeks Spencer's biscuit dough flesh began hardening, his muscles firming, his weight reducing. In a month he scarcely ever felt the taste of metal in his foods. The nausea and abdominal cramps disappeared as though they had never bothered him. And his energy index climbed rapidly, indicating the end of liver sluggishness. His dull eyes now had a sparkle in them and he seemed like a youngish man on the way up.

In this case I used something out of the ordinary to wake up his liver locally, besides the miracle foods and exercises that helped him systemically. It was a hot-cold-hot technique that I'd developed for use in cases of lipomata—what the women call cellulitis. Here it is.

Have two pans of water prepared, one with hot water and one with cold, and a small thick towel in each. Also have a large and heavy Turkish towel, a dry one, at your side. Now do this.

THE HOT-COLD-HOT WAY TO WAKE UP
THE LIVER

Begin with the hot towel over the liver. Rinse it out of its hot water immersion and apply it just below the lower right ribs, which is over the liver area. Keep it there for four minutes, and the towel should be as hot as can be comfortably borne. Then whip if off the liver area and quickly apply the cold towel over the same area. As the towel rinsed out of cold water touches the skin there is a mild shock, which contracts the blood vessels. Keep the cold towel there for only one minute, then off quickly and just as quickly apply the hot towel again for another four minutes, which dilates the vessels and permits the in-flow of fresh blood nutrition. During these four minutes you rinse the towel out of its cold water and have it ready to apply at the end of the four minutes for another one-minute period. Last, you give the liver area a four-minute hot water application and that's all.

It is a 19-minute technique, beginning and ending with four-minute hot applications. Between the hot applications you use one-minute cold towels to the area. While the hot should be quite hot, short of scalding the skin, the cold water should be cooled down by adding ice cubes if necessary. Once you use this technique you will remember it forever. When employed on the genital area, as I have pointed out in other books, it often returns long lost sexual ability.

REHABILITATING A WINO AFTER REFORMING HIM

This was the hot-cold-hot-cold-hot-cold-hot treatment given to Clarence when his disturbed family brought him in, unkempt and unshaven, almost from the gutter to which he had descended after leaving his decent middle-class family. It was after a divorce that was deeply traumatic, which caused Clarence to leave his home and teenage children (who sided with the mother), uncaring about anyone and taking to the wine bottle for escape.

The story was a long one and not worth the retelling. His photo in a newspaper caused the family to find him and try to bring him back. Members of the family had been good longtime patients and they begged me to give their run-down black sheep my best attention.

Much of his liver was damaged from over-drinking. Restoring shot liver cells is always difficult. A lot of brewer's yeast supplied the B vitamins his liver needed. Tomatoes at every meal and in between as snacks gave him needed nutritional support. In addition, radishes in salads stimulated his appetite for food and away from alcohol. Lecithin improved the circulatory flow through his worn-down liver. The 19-minute hot-cold-hot technique awakened and triggered nerve impulses to his liver.

Here, in Clarence's case, I individualized my approach a little. To help ward off his desire for wine or other alcoholic beverages, I kind of manufactured a sweet tooth by giving him a lot of blackstrap molasses and carob, which is obtained at health food stores and tastes like chocolate. When the former gave him loose and blackish stools I knew his liver was pretty well cleaned out and I reduced the daily intake of blackstrap molasses to one tablespoonful.

After trying various drinks I learned that Clarence took to barley water best of all. It appeared to have what his system craved. Since I desired that he drink plenty of fluids to keep his urinary flow going, his family merely boiled whole barley and drained off the water which they cooled down as a drink.

At the start, Clarence was a lanky beanpole of a man with a wrinkled face and spindly bones weighing 110 pounds. Four months later he had filled out to some 150 pounds and had a face so rounded and almost cherubic that few recognized him. Trained in accounting, he went back to working as a CPA, even met a lady he thought of marrying, reentered a good relationship with his estranged children and was altogether a new man.

The "new man" reference is amusing. A year later we met him and his lady at a restaurant. He observed that my drink was a tall glass of tomato juice heavily laden with lemon juice. I recommended it and ordered one for him. When it came he downed it with relish and, retaining the waiter, he extended the empty glass with the remark, "This drink makes me feel like a new man . . . now the new man wants a drink." The waiter took the empty glass and hurried to bring a refill. "Life now is glorious," he said, "as Sarah here can tell you," patting his lady's hand for approval. "Indeed," she affirmed, and laughed merrily. "You can't know how often he tells me the miracle of his life revolves around and tapers down to miracle foods."

SUMMARY—LIST OF FOODS THAT REJUVENATE THE LIVER

Principal foods: BREWER'S YEAST
TOMATOES
RADISHES
LECITHIN (flakes or liquid)

Assisting foods: WHEAT GERM
SUNFLOWER SEEDS
PUMPKIN SEEDS
RASPBERRIES
BROWN RICE
WATERMELON
BARLEY WATER
PEARS
TOMATO JUICE
SOYBEANS

6

Incredible Miracle Longevity Foods for the Pancreas

For the pancreas I have conducted several projects with all proper research conditions observed, and of the various foods researched, the best by a wide margin for the pancreas came out to be blackstrap molasses.

It sounds like just a euphonious phrase, but some foods are in fact so great for certain conditions as to warrant being called miracle foods. Examples are brewer's yeast and tomatoes for the liver, pumpkin seeds for the prostate gland, radishes and raspberries for gall bladder maladies, lecithin for the brain, wheat germ for the heart, cranberries for asthmatic (lung) difficulties, etcetera, etc., etc.

Moreover, even besides the foremost, chief, principal foods that have been known to produce near miracles in maladies of the above mentioned organs, there are others such as sunflower seeds with the rich vitamin A content for the eyes; lecithin which can prevent the formation of gallstones and at times even dissolve the bile cholesterol that is a major constituent of one type of gallstones; soybeans which are so rich in organic utilizable lecithin that they have the property of "liquefying fat" and widening arterial room by dissolving away the clots adhering to inner arterial walls—all of these can be depended upon to work most of the time but do not work all the time.

I had a case once where everything appeared to go wrong although what I was doing was altogether right. He was a white-haired international industrialist who'd made millions through military contracts with our government, but had a deep-seated diabetic condition that even his riches could not help. I gave Emil the proper list of miracle foods headed by blackstrap molasses and assisted by avocado, chlorophyll, cold pressed soya oil and the rest, plus the exercises to align his spine and assure a free flow of power through nerves to his pancreas. He appeared to improve for a time and then, boom!—everything fell apart. There was a genuine recrudescence of his trouble; he once more needed as many daily minims of insulin as before, and he lost a bit of his faith and I wavered in my equanimity.

THE BEST COMBINATION IS
NO COMBINATION AT ALL

Then I saw the problem. I had given the great man a list from which he could choose and assemble the "best foods," but had not reckoned that he would overstuff himself on some and avoid others which he did not relish. He needed a mono-diet program—merely one food at a meal, and as much as he desired of that one food—then his poor pancreas could have a daily rest because any food he ate was compatible with itself and he could not possibly swallow wrong combinations that disagreed with him. The best combination is no combination at all.

For breakfast Emil had only oranges, as many as he wanted. For lunch he had only pumpkin seeds as his protein meal (for he also had a touch of prostate gland trouble and this was the miracle food in such a case), and with the pumpkin seeds he could have a lettuce and cucumber salad because this was neutral and combined with anything except fruit. For dinner he had only a lightly steamed vegetable chosen from among zucchini squash, cauliflower, broccoli or mustard greens. All he desired of any of these one-food-per-meal items—but you can eat only so much of any one food and then it becomes cloying.

Just one week of this and our man was back on track. His need for injecting himself with insulin became progressively less. I sat him down for a long talk that two years later he told me he had never forgotten, a talk which I shall try to reproduce here because I think every diabetic, or anyone who has a loved one with diabetes, should read it and *heed*.

"First off, Emil, here is the bitter truth as I have researched it and learned it. Those with diabetes, especially when they get the disease early in life, are more prone to cancer problems than others, and I have learned how to ward this off. Moreover, there's a history of cancer in your family, which makes what I am about to tell you more important. Are you listening?"

He nodded, very alert and sober.

WHEN CANCER THREATENS

"Two vital protective measures:" I continued. "One, in some unclear way, vitamin A has a kind of insurance against cancer, so I ask you to take a teaspoonful of virgin or Norwegian cod liver oil every night at bedtime without fail, and always at least two hours after eating any food. That's for the best vitamin A fortification outside of sunflower seeds that I can think of. Is that clear?"

"Yes, very," he said.

"Two, it is essential to give your poor fighting pancreas a long daily rest and this is how you do it. Instead of having it labor around the clock by nibbling on protein foods at all meals, you must eat protein items only once a day, best at noon, and thus give the pancreas a 16- to 20-hour rest every day, which it uses in self-repair efforts. From the list I give you of healing miracle foods for the pancreas, you may choose any one or two non-protein items for breakfast and the same for dinner; that is, soups or salads and a few fruits and some steamed vegetables but no protein foods. To normalize your blood sugar levels, you will take everyday a large spoonful of that fabulously helpful black-strap molasses.

"I ask you never to forget the value of blackstrap molasses. It is not only very rich in iron for your essential energy needs but also in organic copper which enables your system to utilize iron. You must also take lecithin daily, and in liquid form I hope, but at least in the form of lecithin flakes along with skim milk. I have never known a person with diabetes or pancreatitis to achieve regenerated health without a rich intake of iron plus daily lecithin supplies."

A PRIMER FOR PROTECTION

"Now let us add the following to the Primer for Protection, Emil. Half an avocado every day for the fatty needs of the body. Green raw vegetables such as parsley, cabbage, spinach and celery liquefied in a blender to supply the chlorophyll you require, say, four ounces of this 'green gold' every other day at least. Cold pressed soya oil (or wheat germ oil) on your daily salad, say, one or two teaspoonsful. Daily exercises—vigorous ones—to keep the power lines open from your spine to your pancreas, and give special attention to the Dowager's Hump because it tends to release nerve pressures in the mid-back, where your trouble tends to lie. And, as a list of foods to choose from, special attention to and very little deviation from the following:

"Bioflavonoid drinks almost daily. Brewer's yeast in your soups and over salads. Brown rice as an occasional starchy food. Soybeans which can be mashed into a paste and used as a spread on a slice of wheat germ toast. Wheat germ as a raw cereal about twice a week. Cooked or canned tomatoes in any desired amount."

This was an intelligent man used to absorbing facts and, to a degree, disciplining himself. Two years later he was in the audience at a lecture I gave in his city, and he came forward after the talk to have a word with me.

"Remember me?" he asked after the ordinary greetings and amenities. "I mean, do you remember my case?"

Of course I remembered and asked him for a fill-in. "In my many travels I have to violate the rules and I'm afraid I do so too frequently," he said a bit sheepishly. "But now I know what to do. Now I don't have to stick that needle into my skin so often. Now I know what are the miracle foods, and where I have to run for cover when I am swamped with trouble."

I waited as he ruminated, his eyes off in space.

"You know, Doctor, many first-rank things happen in a man's life, but there are always one or two of paramount importance. In my life one was my first government contract to sell my product to the U.S. Navy. The other was that list of miracle foods you gave me. I count those two as the chief turning points in my existence."

TWO REASONS FOR HYPOGLYCEMIA

Almost the same, and yet quite opposite in symptoms, was the hypoglycemia of the Canadian chiropractor in her mid-40s. It is held that many millions in our land suffer from low blood sugar, a statistic that may be overblown because the symptoms of hypoglycemia can be confused with a hundred other conditions, since they resemble everything else in the symptomatology manual.

Why do people have low levels of sugar in their blood? There are two good and sufficient reasons. Millions of people have definite, easy-to-find interferences or blockages on the nerve pathways to their pancreas, and this of course, halts the flow of nerve impulses that the pancreas needs for its functions. When a doctor, trained in detecting and releasing such nerve interferences, corrects the nerve pressures, or when the exercises throughout this book do it, there is a better flow of life force, or power, to the pancreas and the organ is able to perform what it is supposed to perform.

Second, the average person consumes enormous amounts of refined sugar (over a hundred pounds of the stuff annually), and this so overworks the pancreas that it *over*produces insulin just as in diabetes it *under*produces insulin. Since insulin converts sugar into simpler, more usable metabolic substances, too much insulin over-converts sugar to below the required levels.

I have never seen even a single case of identifiable hypoglycemia, as in Dr. Kathryn's case, fail to improve when both spinal treatments or exercises were employed, *plus* a daily intake of two tablespoonfuls of blackstrap molasses, several lemons and oranges daily liquefied in a blender for their bioflavonoids, a large quantity of brewer's yeast for the needed B vitamins, barely any starchy food except brown rice for about a month, and *nothing with sugar in it at all.* Along with this the allowable protein foods were soybeans, wheat germ, avocado (because the fatty substance is also useful here), and at least one tablespoonful of liquid lecithin daily.

A MIRACLE MIXTURE

In the case of this chiropractic doctor, what worked immediate wonders was this individualized mixture: a small quantity of liquid lecithin in a dish with half a mashed banana and plain yogurt, this mixture taken about every two hours during the first day or two. The ingredients could be made small or large to suit, so long as all were used. When the doctor also took only tomatoes for breakfast for a week and added both chlorophyll tablets and soya oil to her salads, the results were even more swift and satisfactory.

"Why do those tomatoes do this?" she asked. "Even canned tomatoes?"

"That I do not know," I answered. "But I do know *empirically* that it often produces amazing results, especially in conjunction with the blackstrap molasses and the other foods—and the exercises."

"Will I ever be able to quit those exercises, do you think?" she asked.

"Probably not," I said. "But what's wrong with doing them all your life? You do have a need for *some* activity, you know, and that'll be always."

"Good enough," she answered. "Just knowing that—and those miracle foods—is like finding a gold mine that will keep you all your lifetime."

SUMMARY

Principal food: BLACKSTRAP MOLASSES

Assisting miracle foods: SOYBEANS
                                    CHLOROPHYLL
                                    BIOFLAVONOIDS
                                    BREWER'S YEAST
                                    WHEAT GERM

AVOCADO
LECITHIN (liquid or flakes)
COOKED OR CANNED TOMATOES
SOYA OIL (cold pressed)
BROWN RICE
PUMPKIN SEEDS
COD LIVER OIL
YOGURT

7

Five Foods
That Feed and Restore
the Kidneys

There is at present a great rise in kidney ailments and a great need for knowledge in the matter of how to prolong the life and health of our kidneys.

Since the rising vogue of "shots" for so many human ailments, the poor kidneys have had to filter out the injected foreign agents from the blood, and kidney disease has risen. Even without widespread newer "shots" like the Salk vaccine, the kidneys need to filter and cleanse about two thousand pounds of blood per day—and since the advent of more and more shots for children, I have noted an increased incidence of kidney disease in our young ones.

Beth was a fiftyish schoolteacher with gravel or calculi in her kidneys. Since a siege of blood poisoning in early childhood, she had battled Bright's disease off and on, a worrisome nephritis in the tubules and interstitial tissue of her kidneys. No help was available anywhere for her tingling fingers and toes, her swollen ankles and hands, her unusually dry skin and recurring high blood pressure. No help, that is, until she began on asparagus and raw beet juice, together with dandelion greens, watermelon, and bioflavonoids *plus* a mild program to take pressures off her spinal nerves and eliminate some of her waste products by way of frequent sauna baths.

Usually I am not in favor of saunas, because the sweating is unnatural and I prefer a daily natural sweat from working in the garden under the sun, let's say, or from exercising. But Beth lived in an elegant apartment complex that had sauna facilities, and she found them convenient, so I had her sweat out some of the accumulated wastes twice a week that way.

I have written in another book that raw beet juice has an affinity for human kidneys, or the kidneys have it for beet juice, and that the juice of beets spooned out slowly all day long often fairly sweeps gravel and stones out of the kidneys.

But as a specific miracle longevity food for the kidneys, I must advise asparagus. This is because it contains asparamid, which I have found to be the best kidney cleanser—an entirely natural one with no side effects whatever. Of all foods, only asparagus, I think, is better canned than raw, especially the canned asparagus spears packed in salt-free fluid. So our little teacher was put on a full day of only a spoonful of raw beet juice every five minutes, then asparagus several times a day—even a whole can full of it whirled round in a blender with its own juice as a morning drink.

Besides the five foods mentioned above, the miracle beet juice, asparagus, dandelion greens, watermelon and bio-flavonoids, Beth was advised to drink every day a four-ounce drink of "green gold," which is blended or juiced parsley, spinach, celery and green peppers, because this was, among other virtues, rich in magnesium to help dissolve the kidney stones. Also, for a long while her only allowable protein food was assorted raw nuts (pecans, almonds, cashews) because they also contained the needed magnesium to dissolve the oxalic acid crystals in her kidneys.

Within two weeks the teacher's blood pressure went down, somewhat with the help of raw garlic every day. The tingling in her extremities fairly disappeared and her dry skin took on what she called, "the look of human skin."

Nonetheless Beth complained. There were two reasons. One was that her urine had a strong odor of ammonia, and this frightened her. The other was that she thought her skin and breath reeked of garlic. When I explained that the ammonia smell was normal and physiologically right because of the asparagus she took on board—it proved the asparagus was doing its job—and that soon the system would be garlic-saturated and the "reeking" would cease, her fears were assuaged and she went on with the eating and exercising program plus the sauna baths.

The schoolteacher was a short and chubby person, and the new eating-plus-exercise-plus-saunas schedule firmed her up and brought a weight loss. She held closely to her diet, and was permitted only to choose from among lecithin, boiled onions, carrots both raw and steamed, zucchini squash either raw or steamed, soybeans and whole barley, in addition to the five miracle foods and nuts as her sole protein intake. In five weeks' time the great event happened.

"It's a miracle," she almost screamed over the phone. "This morning I voided my kidneys and heard sounds against the porcelain bowl. It was gravel. Kidney stones. They've washed out!"

She had suffered from an over-acid state and the alkaline effect of the asparagus had neutralized her inner plumbing. It also served as a mild laxative (aperient) and helped her bowels. It had a rich calcium content that helped her to sleep well and provided additional bone strength. The asparagus also lent potassium for Beth's heart. Not least in importance, it provided organic chlorine about which I have this to say.

In the nucleus of every cancer cell there is an odor particle that has been called "the raw stuff of cancer." Chlorine has the world's best known ability to extract odors from anything, even extracting perfume oil essences from porous jars. I have written a research paper on this but for here and now it suffices to say that the daily consumption of asparagus, canned or fresh, is a possible cancer protective that can certainly do no harm.

Its value was again proved in the get-well schedule of Bert, a cynical newspaperman who thought it was all hogwash but tried the beet juice and asparagus program anyway "because what have I got to lose—the conventional folderol didn't help me at all."

Bert was a big bald-headed bruiser of a man who had taken a variety of sulfa drugs that left him with crystals in his kidneys.

"Those pups treat you for one thing and leave you with a worse thing!" he growled. "Why don't medical men give an accounting of the harm they do like anybody else?"

The best way to treat this man was by being equally harsh, I decided. "My program will be tough," I warned, "and if you'll give me a lot of static let's not even start. Find another doctor, Bert, if you want an easy way out. All I can promise you is no side effects—no second ailment in place of the first one as a result of my treatment."

RAW BEET JUICE FOR THE KIDNEYS

He agreed and I put him on raw beet juice for a day. "Don't try to outsmart me and drink this eight-ounce glass of raw beet juice in one gulp," I cautioned him. "The human body isn't geared to this and it will make you very sick. Just swallow a teaspoonful of the beet juice every five minutes or so until you've had all the eight ounces. If your urine turns red, or if you see red in the stool, don't be frightened because that's normal."

He said he had a juicer and could prepare the glassful of juice from fresh raw beets. After the first day he went on a rather heavy schedule of consuming asparagus. For his protein needs, he was limited to three ounces of mixed pecan and almond nuts daily—more than I usually permit, but Bert was a larger than average man. What helped was that a colleague on his paper had read a book of mine and been helped by its advice, which gave Bert confidence because "Charlie is nobody's idiot and if he says he was helped, he was." I sat the big man down and gave him a talk.

"You're in the communicating business and I want you to know something of my work and research findings so that perhaps you can communicate it to others sometimes." He listened and nodded.

"I have discovered that one great virtue of asparagus is that it tends to break up, and often even dissolve, the oxalic acid crystals in the kidneys, and also in rheumatic muscles."

"Great," he interrupted. "Crystals in the kidneys are what those drugs left me with."

"Best of all, Bert, I have found asparagus is a renal *deobstruent*, meaning that it has the property of unblocking kidney blockage. I am going to load you with asparagus plus other miracle longevity foods: watermelon, barley water, whole barley, as your main starchy food for a month or two, mixed raw nuts as the main protein, raw or steamed carrots and boiled onions and dandelion greens for a daily vegetable plate. In your case I will want you to take the following drink as often as you can: a whole can of asparagus spears whirled rapidly in a blender and mixed with an entire lemon for bioflavonoids and apple cider vinegar for hydrochloric acid. This will make a life-extending morning beverage for you. You have a bit of kidney dropsy, I note, and this will help the fluids that collect in your lower limbs, stopping it I hope."

This gruff and rough man was really a dear patient. When he understood the uses and merits of liquid lecithin, and the value of swaying and arching his spine, crawling on hands and knees, doing the wonder-working Primordial Walk, he went at all of it like a man of dedication and was a reasonably well man in six weeks.

"I've never been better fed in my life," he boasted, "and never felt better since football days in college. If all doctors knew about miracle foods and these simple ways of properly aligning the body, most of our hospitals would have to be converted into macaroni factories or something."

SUMMARY

Principal food: ASPARAGUS (canned or fresh)

Also principal: RAW BEET JUICE (sip at five-minute intervals)

Assisting miracle foods: DANDELION GREENS
WATERMELON
BIOFLAVONOIDS

Other helping/healing foods: GARLIC
LECITHIN
BARLEY WATER

WHOLE BARLEY
PECANS AND ALMONDS
APPLE CIDER VINEGAR
ZUCCHINI SQUASH
CARROTS (raw or steamed)
SOYBEANS

8

Extraordinary Miracle Foods for the Urinary Bladder

Watermelon, mentioned earlier in connection with nephritis, which is inflammation of the kidneys (and equally effective in nephrosis, which is kidney degeneration without inflammation), is in my judgment one of the best healing foods for the urinary bladder.

I have found it to be by far the best natural diuretic, and the most dependable, and without any side effects or untoward harm done to the rest of the body. What makes watermelon so effective? It has the ability to wash out of the bladder retained toxins and debris more quickly than anything else I know; anything, that is, without undesirable side reactions.

This was proved by Marilyn, a mother of nine whose embarrassing and exasperating problem of dribbling urine, which she'd been unable to control for two years, was to all purposes cured—entirely halted—by the use of watermelon.

Because Marilyn was also quite obese I had her exclusively on watermelon for two whole days, then for another day on cranberry juice to load the urinary bladder lining with plenty of assimilable vitamin C. Then she went on a mono-diet for a full week, eating only one kind of food at each meal, but as much as she desired of that one food. In her case she did not care to change from oranges for breakfast, tofu (a bean curd) for lunch, along with a lettuce and tomato salad and lemon juice dressing, and plain yogurt with one small banana for dinner. Unlike others she did not find this monotonous and kept to only these foods for seven days, losing 12 pounds in that one week.

The great trick here is the precise manner in which watermelon is used. If eaten in large slices it does not work its magic. To make it serve as a wonderful diuretic one must cut the watermelon into small cubes only a bit larger than sugar cubes and pop one into the mouth all day long about five minutes apart. No other drink is taken, nor is any food eaten during the 24-hour bladder-cleansing program. This schedule somehow "gears" the system to absorbing the watermelon juice drop by drop all day long, and one excretes incredible amounts of urine from the bladder.

Marilyn was assisted in her dribbling problem by several other raw foods after her week on a mono-diet. Peeled raw cucumbers sliced the long way and eaten from the hand—this was her regular snack food between meals. Steamed parsnips are a kind of miracle food in bladder ailments, I have found, so this was a steady vegetable in her case. A teaspoonful of kelp powder was taken at bedtime each day because of a threatening thyroid problem. A large salad plate of almost all the raw vegetables she desired was a daily requirement, with only plain yogurt or lemon juice as a dressing. If obtainable, dulse or Irish moss was also desirable in this case.

Marilyn showed some sugar in her urine from time to time and as a precaution I advised an extraordinary miracle food: Jerusalem artichokes. She had never used Jerusalem artichokes and did not know it had an ingredient curiously akin to the natural insulin manufactured by the human pancreas. Because there is a close relationship between the pancreas and low or disturbed blood sugar levels, I sometimes use Jerusalem artichokes in hypoglycemia. Moreover, this nutritious item can be eaten with frequency where there is a state of muscle weakness. *Note:* It is the fleshy underground stem of the vegetable that is eaten.

Two years later Marilyn brought her eldest daughter into the office for attention and reported that the dribbling had not returned. No more incontinence, no more loss of urine, no more embarrassment. Technically and ethically it could be called a cure.

Next to watermelon, pears that are well ripened are in my opinion the best natural diuretic because they also flush out the urinary bladder in a most satisfactory way. I advise them taken the last thing at night by just about everyone every few months, for we all accumulate contaminants and bladder toxins that should be washed out of the area with regularity. I have found Bartlett pears are best for this purpose, although other varieties do almost as well. Raw cucumbers, parsnips, asparagus, cranberry juice and artichokes are the other miracle foods for the urinary bladder that I have found dependable. The parsnips and Jerusalem artichokes are eaten steamed, of course, rather than raw. And in the matter of cranberry juice, this is not to be confused with the cranberries themselves which act as a kind of bronchial antispasmodic in asthma and other bronchial ailments; the juice does not contain this and is used as a vitamin C-rich diuretic in this context.

THE MAGIC OF WATERMELON AND ASPARAGUS

In the case of Clement, an aging man in the insurance business, merging asparagus with its healing properties for the kidneys with the recommended one-day watermelon program for the bladder worked an authentic miracle. For the past year or so he had risen about a dozen times a night to void urine, and it was not at all a prostate problem in his case. The urinary bladder needed attention. Here was a gaunt elderly man entirely unhelped by conventional medicines reduced to two night risings in a single week and none at all in a month. Except for the monodiet, for which there was no need in Mr. Clement's case, his program was the same as that for the stout mother of nine, Marilyn. In the matter of exercise, however, I did face a large difference. The stout Marilyn could do the swaying and arching of her back on all fours to realign her spine, and she could also do the Primordial Walk with great benefit, but she said her weight prevented her from doing the basket roll on the floor and she refused to run any race on hands and knees. The elderly Clement, on the other hand, did it all—every last exercise—but especially the squat drill.

"I squat down as far as I can and waddle around my yard like an imbecile or monkey," he declared with a big grin. "But then I go to the office feeling like I'm a hundred years younger. I will never let go those miracle foods. Now when I insure anyone's life I tell them about the miracle foods for extra life insurance."

Sometimes there is only a fine line between identifiable kidney trouble and urinary bladder problems, in which case I have found really great results in employing both the watermelon and the asparagus techniques. Together they impart a level of health that I have found is beyond anything for the urinary system available in the pharmacopeia.

This proved itself in the case of the very old doctor who had both Parkinson's disease and an inability to hold back his urine. His wife, a registered nurse considerably younger and much more alert, brought him in and was as solicitous of him as of a helpless baby. She was a precious woman and I directed all program recommendations to her.

"Among these other things," she told me, "my husband, Dr. Herbert, has a deep-seated cold and needs help there." Because she was smart, although medically trained with conventional approaches to colds that I did not approve of, I took the time to give her the actual facts as I had researched them and knew them.

NO CURE FOR THE COMMON COLD

"There is no cure for the cold," I said. "It is a vain hope to search for one. There will never be found any cure for the common cold." This caused her to open her eyes wide, and she bent forward to listen hard.

"The cold itself is the cure," I went on.

"Oh?" she said, a bit disbelievingly.

"Yes, it is. In your body and mine there is a built-in tolerance level for the accumulation of toxins, debris, poisons that may put an end to life. When the body reaches close to the level of tolerance that is inimical to the continuance of life, ah—then the symptoms of a cold appear. The eyes may water and thus wash out the poisons. We sneeze and hurl out the toxins. We cough and expel the pollutants. We have a fever and burn up the waste products. We sweat and expel them that way. This, my dear lady, is the cold syndrome, the symptoms of a common cold. And we've been conditioned by the "do something" medical people to take *things* for a cold, all of which suppress the symptoms. *They push the outgoing poisons inwards.* Some of them pile up in joints that are out of the way of active blood circulation, or in other places, and we have the pyramiding of disease all because we "do something" for a cold, do something to suppress it."

"Judas Priest!" the lady exclaimed. "I've never heard more or better sense. If you are that original in your researches maybe you can come up with original aids for Dr. Herbert's lost urine control, if not for the Parkinson's."

The day on watermelon increased the urine flow for that day but held down the incontinence a little right away. The asparagus appeared to wash out his urinary bladder further. The cranberry juice laid in a base of vitamin C and seemed to rid the bladder of irritating bacteria. I taught her to do the head lift on her spouse and by the fourth day she thought his tremors were less in both hands and feet. The nurse/wife was cautiously enthusiastic.

I encouraged long walks within his limits and capacity. The lunchtime meals of mashed soybeans on whole wheat toast gave him both appetite and energy and he began to get down on elbows and knees to sway and arch his spine. Within two weeks the doctor almost had control of his urine-flow. I thought it time for another wash-out of his bladder and had him do another day on watermelon plus ripe pears at bedtime. By the third week there was no more urinary incontinence and the old doctor even got some flexibility in his body in place of the rigid and peculiar gait that is characteristic of Parkinson's disease.

"Dr. Herbert now has some expression in his face," his wife told me at the end of the month. "He doesn't just stare at me any more, and his speech has speeded up. Do you think there can in fact really be a cure for Parkinson's?"

The old man's food was soybeans and baked potatoes and raw cucumber snacks and salads for the most part. For a change he had a dish of tofu plus about two ounces of mixed pecans, almonds and cashews, all raw. He liked alfalfa tea drinks, which I encouraged, and also Jerusalem artichokes. After a while his weak muscles gave way to strength and he became avid about doing my favorite of all exercises, the Primordial Walk. At the end of ten weeks I discharged him because he was far less palsied than he'd been for years, which indicated that his Parkinson's was arrested, and there was no uncontrolled loss of urine whatever. All this in a man who was nearly ninety years of age.

"You know," he told me that last day in my office, "If I were starting out in the doctoring business I'd want to be your intern and learn all about this miracle food approach instead of my *materia medica*. It beats the world for results."

SUMMARY

Principal foods (2): WATERMELON
                                    RIPE PEARS

Assisting miracle foods: ASPARAGUS
                                         JERUSALEM ARTICHOKES
                                         CRANBERRY JUICE
                                         RAW CUCUMBERS
                                         KELP (or Irish moss)
                                         PARSNIPS
                                         SOYBEANS
                                         BAKED POTATOES
                                         PECANS, ALMONDS, CASHEWS
                                         ALFALFA TEA
                                         YOGURT
                                         TOFU

9

Authentic Health-Restoring Foods for the Prostate Gland

The one great—very great—food for the male prostate gland is a daily two-ounce portion of pumpkin seeds. In the case of very large men, as much as three ounces. PUMPKIN SEEDS ought to be written in capitals, as here. It is so unbelievably important and dependable a natural aid for male readers, particularly those who are middle-aged or older.

Among Gypsy tribes where pumpkin seeds are consumed as commonly as we eat peanuts or popcorn here, and in other countries where pumpkin seeds are snacked on all day long, it is a statistic and fact of life that prostate gland trouble and its associated problems are virtually unknown among middle-aged and elderly males.

I mentioned pumpkin seeds to Colin, a visiting Briton who suffered an obstruction in his urethra, being unable to void urine freely because of prostatic trouble. He was ready for surgery and all for trying anything else first. When I explained that he was out of mechanical adjustment structurally, and was thus unable to properly utilize even the best healing ingredients of the miracle prostate gland foods, this intelligent Englishman understood and bent efforts to correct the misalignment. While consuming pumpkin seeds he also worked diligently at doing the Primordial Walk and basket roll and sway-and-arch exercise for his spinal vertebrae.

When the pelvic bones came into juxtaposition with neighboring structures I explained matters to Colin.

"Pinched nerves in this pelvic area," I told him, indicating the low lumbar area of his spine, "create a problem in the prostatic plexus, which are pelvic nerves that supply the prostate gland and the erectile parts of the penis and also two little sacs where other portions of semen are secreted. That's very important, because now that you're exercising yourself out of this pinched-nerve state, the unblocked nerves are fully feeding the prostate with healing power and the gland can quite properly benefit from the miracle quality of pumpkin seeds plus the other miracle foods: apricots, turnips, cod liver oil for vitamin A, soybeans and pecans and the rest."

Colin asked the right questions and I gave him the right answers.

"Your prostate gland manufactures a thin fluid that goes into forming semen. Your prostate is harder and more swollen than it should be, and this squeezes on the urethral tube through which you eliminate urine, thus blocking the flow. For a healthy prostate a man needs a plenitude of unsaturated fatty acids, and in this, pumpkin seeds are extraordinarily rich. And of all known seeds, pumpkin seeds are richest in organic iron (to give you a burst of natural energy) while also a great source of vitamin B."

All this fascinated our British friend. He was "quite booked for surgery," as he put it, but had never heard any of this about pumpkin seeds, or, indeed, that anything but surgery was good for an ailing prostate gland.

"Look," I told him, "since close to one-third of pumpkin seeds are by weight pure protein of the very highest value, I say to you and to other prostate gland sufferers to stop for a while eating meats and cheeses with their toxic residues, and for about a month consume only a combination of pumpkin seeds, pecan nuts, sunflower and sesame seeds for your single daily protein meal.

"Then also abandon the use of all drinks of whatever nature, even soups and milk beverages of all kinds, and for that one month get all your liquid strictly from peaches, juicy tomatoes and the like. With not a drop of water or milk or other liquids entering your system, and with your consuming plenty of fluids from melons and other fruits and vegetables, the body will profit from a concentration of the healing miracle values in pumpkin seeds, plus the other good proteins and the prostate gland will have its best chance to get well quickly and naturally."

That is the way it happened. I explained to Colin that certain amino acids tended to relieve an enlarged prostate gland and advised the liberal use of foods rich in the helpful amino acids: soybeans, brewer's yeast, peanuts, filberts and fresh corn—all of them well-tested miracle foods for the prostate gland.

The tall, ever-polite and correct English gentleman of some 55 years ate nothing except what was advised, exercised his heart out to correct the framework that was mechanically out of adjustment, and in just over a month his urine "streamed like a water hose," causing him to telephone his surgeon and cancel the "booking for surgery."

"I cannot fathom it," said Colin. "The doctor sounded upset and somewhat insulting, really, as though I'd committed a crime to get feeling so well without his surgery. Could it be, do you think, that he was miffed losing that big surgical fee?"

Pumpkin seeds are also rich sources of pangamic acid, known as vitamin B-15. This is important because these seeds are for that reason helpful in quieting heart pains and also in lowering high blood pressure. I made this clear to Mr. Denis, an austere manufacturing agent who suffered cardiac distress along with his ailing prostate.

"What in your view causes this pesky prostate trouble?" he asked with great dignity.

FREQUENT CAUSE OF PROSTATE TROUBLE

"I will tell you straight out what causes it most often *in my view*," I said, stressing the last words. I spaced my words so that my speech rhythms were offered with equal dignity, intending to humanize the man a little by being forthright about sex-related prostatic disease.

"It's very often from having sex too long or too often."

"What!" he said, uncomfortably.

"Yes. Let me explain. The prostate gland is a delicate little thing and it works hard to manufacture a fluid that thins down the male semen; without it semen might flow as slowly as glue."

"Yes—what then?" he encouraged, though a bit stiffly.

"Whenever the male is aroused, the gland starts working. If he has sex and finishes in proper time the prostate gland, having done its job, quits making prostatic fluid to thin down any more semen and takes a rest. But—note this, please—if the man stretches out the sex act; if he tries to prolong it out of reason and maintains his erection so long that he squeezes every ounce of extended pleasure out of the sexual union, then the little gland overworks. It becomes inflamed from overuse. When swollen, it squeezes down on the urinating tube that goes through it, blocking and impeding the urinary flow. That's why you have trouble voiding urine. You see?"

"I see," he said, and promptly changed the subject. But my words had taken hold. I recalled that the Bible says "the Word never returns void." He followed directions in every last detail. "Tell me precisely what I must do," he said, and he meant it.

I recommended brown rice and wheat germ and pumpkin seeds, not entirely for his prostate gland but also to quiet the pains in Mr. Denis's heart.(See Chapter 1 for details on lecithin, garlic, blackstrap molasses and other heart foods.) Every day he rode a bicycle upside-down while lying on his back. He rocked on the floor in a basket roll and did the Primordial Walk that helped so many people get back into mechanical alignment from their structurally distorted, out-of-adjustment state. He ran races on hands and knees and did the valuable diaphragmatic breathing (panting with hands raised), thus reoxygenating himself. In less than two months the man had neither heart pains nor urinary problems. I told him that he must continue at least one-half hour a day of exercising for the rest of his life, considering the sedentary character of his work, and he agreed.

"I understand," he said. "Doing all that keeps me in good alignment so that I can utilize the inherent values of the miracle foods." Truly, the man had grasped the essentials of being well.

I met him some years later at a baseball game and he was yelling his head off, looking a dozen years younger.

"I'm in fine fettle," he declared. "And, you know what," he said leaning toward me conspiratorially, "I know about sex now—about having it and finishing with it, not extending it forever."

Another healthifying and really great miracle food for prostate ailments is that which contains vitamin E. Foods in the class of wheat germ and lecithin and soybeans are particularly desirable. As in Mr. Denis's case, and in that of Wilbur, an energetic tennis buff, these foods rich in vitamin E for the prostate gland at the same time usually brought about the cessation of heart discomforts, shortness of breath and the like.

Wilbur was the only tennis enthusiast in a family that avoided such strenuous activities because of a history of heart problems. But Wilbur, in his mid-40s, prided himself on being "muy macho" despite warning periods of shortness of breath and chest discomforts. It was not until he also developed prostate gland problems that he came to me for that plus his heart symptoms. The employment of wheat germ, soybeans and other foods rich in vitamin E and lecithin, plus garlic and blackstrap molasses and sunflower seeds—all this was not enough to make significant changes, so I had to stop the tennis.

"Listen, Wilbur," I began, "when you stand on two bathroom scales, or in front of a string suspended from the ceiling, your body weighs unevenly and measures out lopsided. You must quit tennis because it is a unilateral activity; it develops one side of the body to the exclusion of the other as do other sports such as bowling, horseshoe pitching, to a large extent baseball, etc. What you need is a two-sided activity, a bilateral sport such as rowing, swimming, volley ball, walking and such, where you do not exercise one side of the body at the expense of the other. Is that clear?"

He nodded and said "Yes," but he didn't like it.

"I will give you plenty of drills to work off your energy and at the same time put your misaligned body that is out of adjustment back into a non-lopsided shape. Plenty of rocking in a basket roll, the Primordial Walk anytime you like until it tires you, racing on hands and knees, riding an imaginary bicycle upside-down, swaying and arching your backbone and doing the Dowager's Hump and waddling in a deep squat position. All this will tire you. And it will at the same time tend to rid you of offside nerve pressures. And that will enable your digestive organs to utilize in full the miracle values for the prostate and heart in the soybeans and wheat germ and the other healthifying foods. Again, is that clear?"

"For how long must I do this? How long away from tennis?"

"For a month or two. Perhaps longer. Maybe forever. I do not know. But this I do know, Wilbur. If you go back very strenuously to tennis or any other one-sided activity it will again, with your structural pattern already set in that direction, throw you into bad health."

It was difficult for him to accept it. Wilbur had been raised in a family of wealth that indulged him; it was hard for him to deny himself anything.

"I don't make the rules, my boy," I said sternly. "I only interpret them and carry them out." I paused to let this sink in. "If you enjoy bad health enough to let your prostate and heart become sick, I will enjoy seeing you again and again and again."

That did it. He grinned and said, "You'll never have to see me again, not for this." And he meant it. Although he played tennis on and off lightly and casually, he never again went into tournament play. When I encountered him years later he said, "Tennis is great but with my improved heart I have no heart for it. And I enjoy being free of urinary prostate sickness more than I enjoy tennis anyway."

SUMMARY

Principal food: PUMPKIN SEEDS (raw, unsalted)

Assisting miracle foods: SOYBEANS
PECANS
APRICOTS
TURNIPS
DAILY TEASPOON COD LIVER OIL
FILBERTS
SUNFLOWER SEEDS
LIQUIDS EXCLUSIVELY FROM JUICY
FRUITS
PEANUTS

FRESH CORN

WHEAT GERM OIL (one teaspoon daily)

SESAME SEEDS

BREWER'S YEAST

BROWN RICE

LECITHIN (liquid or flakes)

WHEAT GERM CEREAL

RAW GARLIC

BLACKSTRAP MOLASSES

10

Some Miracle Foods That Recondition the Uterus

Almost every other woman who enters a doctor's office has some uterine problem, small or serious. It is either cramping at menstrual times, or underflowing, or overflowing, or not having the periods often enough, or too often, etcetera. Consequently, for years I sought to help the ailing womb, testing different foods and programs, trying vitamin and mineral combinations or intensified pelvic exercises, seeking fasting and bathing and abdomen-churning, among other things, that promised relief or cure for the problems of the female human nesting place for future generations—the womb.

My first success many years ago came with a case of endometritis, an inflamed condition of the lining of the womb. Then I discovered that many uterine problems were glandular in origin, and that these, like most of the others, were greatly helped by a simple bioflavonoid drink.

A bioflavonoid drink? What's that? Well, it is an unbelievably simple beverage made merely by cutting up an entire lemon or two, skin and pulp and all, and whirling it around with some distilled water in a juicer or blender. If too sour, an entire orange may be added, or even a bit of raw honey. When this was sipped (never gulped down rapidly), either cool or warm, there was something in the tissue between the skin and fruit, it seemed, that abated the inflammation of the uterine lining and aided other dysfunctions of the womb, especially if liberal bioflavonoid drinks were taken along with the various self-aligning body exercises that constituted the Miracle Health Promoter M.

Jennie, a middle-aged lady who served as cook-housekeeper in a large nearby home, reported such verifiable wonders soon after starting on bioflavonoid drinks plus the daily movements of Miracle Health Promoter M. Later, there came other cases with congestive dysmenorrhea and even spasmodic dys-menorrhea where the uterine contractions produce severe pains, cases of amenorrhea or insufficient menstrual flow at irregular intervals, cases of metrorrhagia or too copious blood loss from nonmalignant, but glandular (hormonal) causes—all were helped by the bioflavonoid approach, together with the knee-chest position for several daily five-minute rest periods and the other structure-straightening drills. But Jennie's problem was a kind of menstruation every two weeks instead of every 28 days, and growing worse as she approached menopause. The loss of blood was great, and it both weakened and frightened her.

I told Jennie to get down on the carpet on her hands and knees, or elbows and knees, for a frequent rest period during the day, to churn her lower abdominal muscles in and out while in this position, and to follow this with a cup full of warm or cool bioflavonoid drink, explaining how to make it. "It's the yellowish tissue which divides the sections of the lemon, I think, that provides the bioflavonoid riches," I explained, "but I am not really sure. What I am sure of is that it can do no harm and may produce much good."

In the beginning the nice, very cooperative lady blended both lemons and oranges—skin, seeds, pulp and all—in a juicer and took a four-ounce drink every hour on the hour. Then she used fewer oranges and eventually lemons alone, together with the distilled water. She suffered a malpositioned uterus, which many females have because we live in this up-and-down vertical state, resisting the down-thrust of gravity all the time, and the daily knee-chest position helped get this right while the bio-flavonoid drinks appeared somehow to tighten the suspensory ligaments attached to the uterus. Later I found that women with a womb that was tipped either forwards or backwards from the normal position were equally helped by the same program.

Within three weeks Jennie was making a mixture of six lemons plus one or two grapefruits and a half gallon of water every morning as the day's supply. She got on her back and while lifting her knees to the chest hugged herself into a small basket and rolled from side to side with vigor a few times every day. She did a lot of what I called the Primordial Walk, traversing the large basement floor on hands and feet (not hands and knees), which tended to strengthen and align the entire body. The result was that the expected mid-month period did not come. At the next regular period the flow was only moderately excessive. By the third month Jennie was entirely well.

When I saw Jennie several years later she had gone through the menopausal state with barely any hot flashes or other discomforts, had not at this time any periods or even staining, and was still taking an occasional bioflavonoid drink "for safety's sake."

"Why not?" she asked. "Anything that made me so healthy in three months is better than coffee or tea, no?" I agreed heartily.

AMAZING HEALING DRINK FOR MENSTRUAL PROBLEMS

The bioflavonoid drinks do their best magic, however, when taken along with other "helping" foods which patients came to call "amazing healing foods"—foods such as kelp and lecithin and blackstrap molasses, listed at the end of this chapter.

This I found out when treating Carol, a woman of 42 with almost complete amenorrhea, or absence of menstrual flow, which was the exact opposite of Jennie's condition. When Carol, who was only five feet four inches but weighed 170 pounds, took a four-ounce bioflavonoid drink every hour during ten of her daily waking hours, she began to spot a little but nothing more. By more vigorous attention to the frequent rest periods in the knees-and-elbows position and the Primordial Walks, which reversed gravity, her menstrual flow increased a little more. But then, when the other healing foods were added the whole uterus seemed to become reconditioned and Carol's menses became small and short-lived but regular.

When the second period came, following Carol's start on our program of bioflavonoid drinks, other helper-healing foods, and the drills of the Miracle Health Promoter M, the stout little patient was pleased but not yet sure of results. Twenty-eight days later the menstrual flow was greater, and a month after that it came in full normal flow.

"I've gained a fringe benefit, Dr. Morrison," she said to me with eyes aglow. "In these four months I've gone down to a firm 145 pounds. Maybe it's because I drink so much of the bio-flavonoid drink that I eat less, or whatever . . ." she broke off, not really knowing to what she could attribute her all-round success.

It was then that Carol told me that a young woman who worked alongside her and suffered "fearful cramps every month" joined her every day in the self-aligning exercises and the "sourish lemony drinks," as she called them, "And would you believe it," said Carol, "my friend Jessie got rid of her cramps even without coming here to see you!"

SUMMARY

Principal food: BIOFLAVONOIDS (whole lemon with distilled water, warm or cool, with whole orange if desired)

Assisting healing foods: SOYBEANS (whole or mashed)
LECITHIN (liquid or flakes)
BLACKSTRAP MOLASSES
KELP (powder or tablets)
SESAME SEEDS
VITAMIN C (2 grams daily)
VITAMIN E (400 to 800 I.U. daily)

11

A Half Dozen Foods That Work to Rehabilitate Arthritic Joints

Bone meal is the one most important food, I think, in cases of arthritis. If it is true that more than twenty million Americans have some form of arthritis, then twenty million of us ought to be consuming bone meal every day.

It does not seem to matter much whether the ailment, as diagnosed, is rheumatoid arthritis or osteoarthritis or arthritis deformans or any of the ten or a dozen other types. In all cases I am sure it is the result of errors in metabolism—errors that can be corrected and changed by two things: miracle foods that are healers for arthritis *plus* light drills or exercises that work to reshape the body structurally; that is, put the misaligned arthritic body back into a state of mechanical adjustment.

The loss of bone minerals that is seen in arthritis can be replaced in most cases by daily use of either powdered bone meal or bone meal in tablet form. In those who suffer from any of the forms of arthritis or neuritis, bursitis, gout or what is nonspecifically labeled rheumatism, a near-incredible magic is perfomed by taking a variety of healthifying foods headed by bone meal. Aches in muscles and pains in joints lessen in an unbelievably short time, usually to the surprise of sufferers who had formerly depended on drugs that did not help adequately, besides offering a host of side effects.

The tall visitor from Texas, Big Mike, told me that he had rheumatoid arthritis largely because, said he, "arthritis runs in my family." Many lay people and even some doctors believe that this is so—and there is evidence to verify it. It has been observed that in certain families whenever one gets sick it is heart trouble that takes hold. In other families lung or bronchial problems seem to attack their members whenever any sickness at all descends on them. In still other familites it is kidney dysfunction or glandular trouble or even cancer that seizes the members if and when they get sick at all.

Big Mike had come to California for a long vacation mixed with a desire to get at that arthritis that plagued and pained him daily. In college and afterward he had been good at tennis, so he checked into the swank local beach and tennis club where he hoped to regain former skills and also "bake out" his painful joints.

But sunning and surfing alone did not help. Even the sauna and whirlpool baths at the club availed nothing. He came into the office, smiling through his pains, with a doleful story.

But the big Texas wheeler and dealer was surprised to learn that over the years of practice and research projects I'd come across some half dozen foods that frequently promised miracles for the arthritics, and this went for not only rheumatoid arthritis but seemingly for all other varieties. Despite the man's wealth and far-flung business interests, and his willingness to spend large sums to regain health, the good-natured outflowing Texan had heard nothing like this to cheer and gladden him. His bubbling good humor engulfed all of us in the office.

When he played but a few sets of tennis he developed a painful tennis elbow. Since college football days he'd had a "trick knee" and to this day his knees hurt with almost every step. He had tripped over a coil of rope on his sailboat and his ankles gave him unrelieved misery. Yet he smiled, was bright-eyed with intelligence and laughter, asked questions and was avid to learn all I had discovered about arthritis in a period spanning half a century.

RELATIONSHIP OF BODY MECHANICS TO HEALTH

Because the man knew mechanics I sat him down for a small lesson in *body* mechanics, unwittingly paraphrasing a great medical book called "Body Mechanics in Health and Disease."

"Your body is not too unlike an automobile," I told him, "I know that doctors would have us believe that we are very complicated machines difficult to keep running healthily, but it is not so. We need to understand only two things, really. One—see that the bodily machine is structurally in alignment, for any machine that is out of adjustment can't be expected to work correctly. Two—feed the machine with the right ingredients: proper foods in the case of the human machine and the right grease or oil or lubricants when such are normally meant to go into nonliving machines. You would not pump water, milk or orange juice into your gas tank, would you? Well, curiously enough, I'd not like your taking milk or citrus juice or even very much water on board your human machine either."

This had Big Mike's attention. He could see the wisdom of not pouring milk or fruit juice into his gas tank—but not to pour milk or orange juice, or even much water into his stomach? This was too much.

"I've never even heard such a thing, Doc," he exploded, smiling withal. "Not even milk or water? Aren't you, forgive me, off the deep end a little?"

He really wanted to know. So I told him.

"Milk doesn't work for people, Mike," I said. "I know that the conventional wisdom has it that milk is a perfect food, or a near-perfect food, and that no one ever outgrows the need for milk, and similar euphonious misdirections, but I disagree. Bone meal supplies the needed calcium for bones and joints in exactly the correct proportions with other mineral elements to prevent fractures and the like, while milk, especially when pasteurized, can lead to a porous state of the long bones, a serious condition known as osteoporosis, a kind of softening of the bones.

"It has been determined in controlled tests that bone meal is a far better source of calcium than milk ever was. Milk gives humans all kinds of allergies, but bone meal doesn't. Bone meal always helps—never harms—human bone tissue. Since nearly one hundred percent of our entire skeletal frame is calcium, bone meal (being the richest and most absorbable kind of calcium known), is a life-extending food that should be universally used and should certainly be on every arthritic's bill of fare."

With such new knowledge in nutrition, Big Mike went at his program with enthusiasm, even avidity. One thing troubled him, for he followed a former doctor's advice to drink water copiously.

"What's the story on water?" he asked. "And on fruit juices also, for I guzzle a lot of that too."

SIP . . . NEVER GUZZLE

"Guzzling, by the way, is forbidden," I said quickly. "It's a large trouble with milk, along with other faults that I think milk has as a human food. Milk is protein food mostly—a fluid protein. And fluids are guzzled. They are poured down the throat in a torrent. Your very human stomach simply doesn't have the enzymes to start metabolizing proteins coming down in a gushing stream rather than in one little bite or drop at a time. Juices also should be sipped rather than guzzled, but in arthritis cases I much prefer their taking the needed vitamin C from rose hips or acerola berries or plain ascorbic acid rather than by way of citrus fruits. The juices irritate and accentuate the pains, I have found.

"As to water," I explained, "in my own family we use a water-distilling machine plus a handy little *water-washing* outfit that attaches to the faucet and filters out through charcoal, most of the pollutants. Thus we avoid taking into our systems such undesirable chemicals as chlorine, sodium fluorides, inorganic lime deposits that tend to pile up in human joints as arthritic bumps, and so on and on. For drinking purposes we use only distilled water. For cooking and such we employ the water-washing contraption. In this way we bypass the undesirable substances that would otherwise get inside to clog up the inner plumbing."

Mike liked the reference to inner plumbing. It was his kind

of talk. But he had read widely about arthritis and knew more than most lay people about related matters.

"Forgive me, Doctor," he said, "but if you take only distilled water into your body wouldn't you be leaching out the minerals that your system needs? If you distill away all those minerals in ordinary water, can't you build up one big devastating problem?"

"True, Mike. Almost true," I admitted.

"Almost? How almost?"

"Well, you'd be eminently right if you drank only distilled water and never anything else with plenty of minerals in it. But I will counsel you to consume fluid-bearing papaya with wonderful papain to help digest away uneliminated protein accumulations in your body, and melons, which are full of the best, purest water known to man and also rich in the minerals that your body needs. Also consume juicy tomatoes, and watery peaches and pears, and strawberries which contain natural salicylates in them (salicylic acid is the active ingredient of aspirin, Anacin and similar pain-killing drugs), did you know that? And for a quick drink after a tennis game, to replace the lost fluid, I'll recommend a large slice of watermelon that's full of needed minerals—and can you think of anything more watery than that?"

He saw the sense of this at once, and agreed.

HEALTHIEST WAY TO REPLACE BODY FLUIDS

"But that's only part of it," I continued. "After a sweat brought on by tennis or a sauna bath, you don't replace the lost toxemic fluids with disease-laden faucet water or with soda pop or beer or such. In place of the waste products you sweated out, you put in the purest kind of desirable fluids that have been refined and purified in nature's laboratory—the purest anywhere on earth. You change your blood chemistry thereby. Talk about chemotherapy! This way you healthify yourself decently, and scientifically."

From his concentrated posture, sitting foward in his seat and soaking it all up, I felt this serious healthseeker would not soon forget what he'd heard. I returned to the main thought.

"Bone meal contains the kind of appropriable calcium your arthritic body needs. And the calcium that the body so readily absorbs and utilizes also promotes sleep. It firms up loose gum tissue; it should be used by children because of its value in tooth formation. You see what a new world of rich natural health you can enter by learning and heeding all this?"

"Are there other foodstuffs besides bone meal that are as rich, or almost as rich, for my condition?"

"Yes, Mike. You'll have a list of them. For maladies of the joints, my studies have shown that alfalfa also supplies calcium for the muscles and bones. It was discovered centuries ago by Arab peoples who dubbed it "Great Father of Foods" (Al-Fal-Fa) and I recommend it to you either as a tea or taken in tablets—as many as a dozen a day. Nothing but good there, no possible harm or side effects. And then there's a great fruit: *cherries.* Would you believe that cherries have helped even serious gout when nothing else could? Anything as good as cherries, and more helpful than any drug."

"This is great. Really great information, sir," he said tensely. "I've got a lot to tell those good ole' boys in Texas, especially my colleagues."

"Then here's the story to tell them, Mike. Two research people in your own state worked on this study and found that when eating from half a pound to a pound of cherries in the morning, and nothing else until mid-afternoon, astonishing improvement was seen and felt by very hurting gouty patients. The cherries were also extraordinarily helpful in general muscular rheumatism. Following the program for a month or so, consuming solely cherries as the breakfast food, nearly all were improved and many were entirely cured. And in addition to this, there is yogurt that supplies the arthritis victim with calcium plus those precious lactic acid bacilli. And blackstrap molasses yields the sufferer as much as 50 milligrams of valuable pyridoxine to a single tablespoonful. Moreover, there is asparagus to neutralize away the acid condition in rheumatic ills, and nuts (especially pecans, raw and unsalted) that have had a godsend effect on all types of arthritis. So who needs drugs?"

"Yessirreee," he said enthusiastically. "And who needs to be told about such things? I do! All my friends and fellow workers do. Nobody among my friends or acquaintances knows any of this at all. I have a lot to tell them in Texas."

"There's one more very important integer in this equation," I told him. Then I spelled out for the dear man the crux of the all-encompassing healthifying program. "For the body to be able to absorb the miracle values out of these healing foods, and to utilize them *in the cells* of the ailing body, it must be in good mechanical adjustment so that the various organs can do the job for which they were created. Listen well to this."

"I'm listening," said the big man, leaning forward in his chair.

"No machine that is out of adjustment can be expected by reasonable people to work well. A machine that is out of alignment cannot do its work properly or function normally. This is a factor in health restoration that the dominant medical profession has not taken into account; they attend to the chemistry but not to the mechanical rightness of sick people, so note how sickness is awash in the land and all the great degenerative diseases grow, rather then diminish." I paused to let it soak in. "I am going to tell you how to get your body back into good proper *workable* alignment by a few well-researched movements or exercises. Then, with all the bodily parts where they should be—in mechanical adjustment—they can do the job they were intended to do, they can absorb and utilize the miracle longevity foods and you can get well in the full, all-embracing sense."

"Makes sense," said Mike. "What then, must I also do mechanically to get back to all-round health?"

I showed him how to measure and test himself for mechanical distortions and structural misalignments. I explained that when the body is in a mechanically right position, and we feed it with what it needs for its job, then health follows naturally because the tendency of the body is toward health, just as gouged flesh or a cut finger heals itself naturally. He understood that that was the way to rehabilitate arthritic joints, and he understood why the reigning healing profession did not help arthritic cases—they looked after the chemical side and nothing else.

"Now I see," he said. "I understand why you said getting well isn't as complicated as the doctors would have us believe. I'm your man, Doctor."

THE BODY'S CHEMICAL FACTORY VS.
MECHANICAL STRUCTURE

By declaring that he was my man, he meant that he would follow all the needed directions, and I took him at his word. What I told Big Mike to do was for the most part what I have used in almost every case of arthritis because they are universal directions that help them all. This man had suffered long enough, and had read enough about his ailment that he could rattle off the matters of ankylosis, exostosis, arthritic spicules, epiphyses, scolioses—he knew them all. But he did not know, and was never told, that if the body was structurally out of adjustment there would likely be pinched nerves and that would interfere with the proper flow of vital impulses and fluids which make his machinery and plumbing work properly. In that case, I pointed out to him, it did not matter much what else he did or didn't do; if he failed to get his body into correct functional alignment *as a machine,* all other aids were at best only temporary and could not make for lasting health.

"You were born with a complete chemical factory," I said to him. "At birth your little body already knew how to make insulin, adrenalin, pepsin, cortisone, hydrochloric acid and enzymes and the rest. But you were not born with complete or adequate mechanical equipment. At birth you could not even sit up, much less stand, balance, walk, run, heave and lug and tug and strain as you now do every day. As you adjusted to the tasks that life imposed on you, you often *strained your bodily machinery out of adjustment* (just think of all the jars and falls and impacts you have sustained in all your years), and with a body out of adjustment you just cannot reasonably expect it to function normally. Yet conventional MDs do not study this, cannot write prescriptions for this that would enrich pharmaceutical companies, have no idea how to treat this. Any wonder that you and other arthritics remain sick?"

He did not know how to measure himself for structural misalignments. When I showed him how to do this and he was able to check his progress all by himself, he understood that the underlying dedication of my professional life was to teach the sick how to bypass doctors, drugs and hospitals, how to listen to the wisdom of their own bodies, how to help the body do its own natural thing, which is to get well, for the tendency of the human body is to mend its damages just as it heals its cuts or bruises. Ben Franklin was right when he said, "Nature cures but the doctor pockets the fee."

Most of all, now he understood that there were foods that were seemingly just meant to heal and rehabilitate swollen painful joints, and that the miracle properties resident in such foods could best be utilized by the sick body only when the structure of that body was in proper structural adjustment, not suffering misalignments.

"I will sure and certain put these things together for those ole' boys back home," he promised me when he left as a truly renewed, non-hurting, life-enjoying man. "Life nowadays is really a bowl of cherries," he grinned, opening a sack in his hand and displaying a large quantity of big red cherries. "Now it really and truly is."

SELF-MEASURING TESTS FOR HEALTH AND SICKNESS

Here are the instructions which I gave him, and which he followed, that made the big Texan a new man and that over the years have worked near-miracles for many, very many, arthritis sufferers.

First, stand nude in front of a mirror and note the level of both shoulders. Is one shoulder an inch or two lower than the other? Write on a handy reference card: Left shoulder two inches lower than right. (This must be why the tailor puts in a shoulder pad—to make me look even.)

Second, drop your hands down with open fingers against your naked thighs and note if the arms are longer on one side than on the other. Make a written note of what you see, so that you will have a point from which to measure later as you get back into structural alignment.

Next, place both open palms on the upper crests of your hips and note if one is higher than the other, and note it.

Next, does one shoulder blade stick out farther than its opposite number, as seen in profile from the side?

Now, as you turn your head to left and right as far as you can without undue strain, can you tell if you have equal mobility in both directions or can you not turn as far one way as the other? You may discover that the chin turns to within two inches of the left shoulder but only to within four inches of the right shoulder, which means vertebral strains and possible nerve pressures that you have lived with for years without knowing it.

Now you stand on two little ordinary bathroom scales with feet equidistantly apart and note if you weigh the same on both sides. You should. But if you are 200 pounds (as in Mike's case) and register 110 and 90 instead of 100 on each side, or even a worse lopsidedness, you get a graphic indication of how misaligned you are. Since memory is fickle but paper never forgets, write it down.

Finally, this self-test to inform you, and possibly shock you, how central or offside you really are structurally. Hang a string from the ceiling with a plumb-bob or other weight holding it down. Stand in front of it (facing the full length mirror) with the string exactly between your ankles, and note as your eyes go upward if the string bisects your body precisely. Does the string cut exactly between the calves of your legs, between your knees, the middle of the pubic bone or triangle, the navel, the middle of your breastbone, the central point of your chin and the exact point of your nose and thence upward through the middle of your forehead? Surprise, surprise! Often the string, instead of going straight upward from its place between the ankles, will wander a little (or a lot) off center to the left or right knee, then the nipple, shoulder tip and even miss the head altogether. It is as if your car were in a collision and now drags itself offside, using extra energy to stay in mid-path. It shows that with every step you are *leaking energy* trying to keep yourself upright. This you would not be aware of by any conventional medical examination. Yet it is something you must know if you are to be able to pull yourself back into alignment and enable your system to utilize the foods that can rehabilitate and heal.

Still another self-test for structural distortions is done by using the string sideways. Stand alongside it so that the string is lined up with the point of either your right or left ankle. Now, as your eyes follow the string upward, it should cut through the midway side of your knee-joint, then the middle of your hip-bone, the exact tip of your shoulder on that side, the opening of your ear, finally up through the front-to-back middle of your cranium. But does it? Having tested hundreds of cases I can tell you that in most cases the distorted body wants to lean forward of the string, as though there is a built-in desire to go back to the allegedly primordial position of our ancient ancestors.

Now, having done these measurements (which are trying only the first time), your next step is deliciously simple and logical. Measure yourself before any favorite sport or exercise, then immediately afterward. If the tennis game or Primordial Walk or any other activity made you measure out more nearly even—that is, if what you did put you more closely into alignment—that proves it is right for you and you should do more of it. If the jogging or race on hands and knees or baseball game or golf made you measure out worse than before, then that's the signal to quit that activity. You can test yourself. You bypass the doctor. You know where you are going and what to do about it.

Big Mike was an avid bowler as well as a tennis buff, and it was his custom to quaff large quantities of orange juice after the games in the belief that they were healthful. I explained in somewhat greater detail the effects of citrus juice, and also a little more about milk.

"You already know, Mike, that I cannot countenance milk in your case; it produces more allergies than almost any other food—note how pediatricians are kept busy grappling with the various untoward effects of milk in babies' formulas. Now, just as milk is natural for the calf but not for humans (and the signal is that when the human baby has grown teeth with which to chew more substantial fare, even its own mother's milk should be avoided), and just as tap water is forbidden because it is too laden with pollutants, your orange juice is to be avoided for another good reason. It is a citrus fruit, which leaves an alkaline ash in the human digestive process and slows you down. It makes you draggy. It tends to rob those energies which I prefer to save inside your organism for healing purposes. Yes, oranges and lemons and other citrus items are acid outside the body but the end result inside the body is the opposite—an alkaline ash. That's fine for growing children; they already have too much energy and need to be held down, and it is good for developing teeth. But in adults an alkaline ash makes for listlessness and tends to increase pains in joints and muscles. Adults don't need to be held down, they need to be energized. So instead of your milk or orange juice or tap water I ask you to sip frequently, never quaff or guzzle, fresh carrot juice that is raw and alive with its wonderful content of immediately utilizable vitamin A. Then at mealtimes if you must have fluids to wash down each mouthful, your ticket is a piece or two of fresh watermelon, or seedless grapes when watermelon is not in season."

Then I told Mike something that I believe made the greatest change in not only his health, but in his enthusiasm for the entire natural healing program as opposed to his former drug-taking routine.

"Since tennis and bowling are your hobbies, Mike, I have this plan by which you participate with me in your return to health. You measure your distortions on the two scales, and with a string suspended from the ceiling *before each game,* and you thus note how you stack up as a mechanical machine. Then you do the same *after* each game and tell me what difference you observe."

He reported terrifying results. Before the games his 200 pounds showed 90 on the right and 110 on the left. After two sets of tennis he weighed 85 and 115. "Wow! Tennis isn't for me," he complained.

"That's because it is a one-sided sport," I explained. "So also is bowling."

"And I'm at those billiards tables at the Beach Club every chance I get," he added. "Is pool playing off limits too?"

"Well Mike, suppose I deputize you to find out if it's good or bad. Be your own doctor for this test. Measure yourself before and after an hour of billiards, and you'll know. If it is bad, the figures will show it. Then I can help you into a first-class, sensible solution."

"What's that?" he wanted to know.

TRY LEFT-HANDED SPORTS FOR HEALTH

"Reverse it. Play everything left-handed for a while."

I ordered him to force himself through a game of bowling left-handed, then see how he weighed out and measured up. Do the same with billiards, then with a set or two of tennis done entirely with the left hand.

"Note where the string bisects your body," I told him. "Make a rough drawing or sketch of how you line up, or how far askew you have gone by the various strains and stresses and falls and jarring impacts you've sustained in your lifetime. Be aware of the weight differences on the two bathroom scales and note how far off center you are both before and after some left-handed bowling or a set of tennis played left-handedly."

He did this faithfully. When he weighed out after a game at 95 and 105 instead of 85 and 115, he was impressed. He forced himself to play with the left hand in order to even up the right-and-left development of his body and for the first time realized how little our doctors knew about human structural importance—and how little was generally known about sick human beings being out of alignment to the detriment of their health. Being now aware of this, he noted the level of his ear-lobes: that now they were more nearly level with each other whereas before the right was lower than the left. He saw his low shoulder come up and could hardly believe his eyes. Measuring himself before the string, both frontally and laterally, he saw every day that his structural framework was more nearly in alignment. And he understood what few medical patients ever do: that when the body is mechanically in correct situs it is able to utilize *with the least effort or interference* the miracle foods to heal his ailing organs.

As a guide for all his future, Mike pasted the following list on his morning shaving mirror and adhered to the recommendations almost to the letter.

THE GET WELL AND STAY WELL LIST

Raw Foods: For two or three months, insofar as you can, eat only raw foods, or at least a preponderance of raw foods in your diet. People who have a much lower incidence of arthritis eat only or mostly raw foods. Seventh-Day Adventists, eat no meat but eat a large variety of raw vegetables and fruits and have almost a 90 percent lower incidence of all kinds of arthritis. The Hunza people who eat cooked food only about a dozen times a year (on special festive occasions) do not even know about arthritis according to medical researchers who have lived among them. In research projects, *arthritis has been induced in animals by giving them only cooked foods.*

Drinks: During this two- or three-month period drink no tap water, no milk or fruit juices from citrus fruits, but mostly freshly prepared carrot juice, about four 12-ounce glasses a day if possible, sipped slowly and never poured down the esophagus rapidly. Occasionally such fruit juice drinks as those from watermelon are permitted. If thirst assails you between meals, suck the pure fluids out of a ripe tomato or eat a peach, persimmon, ripe pear, or plum. At mealtimes, if fluids are needed to wash down each mouthful, take small quantities of watermelon.

Bone Meal: For quick benefits to bone and joint tissues take several bone meal tablets or about two teaspoonfuls of bone meal powder daily, the latter sprinkled over salads and soups or stirred into a drink. The dosage here may be more or less, for bone meal is a food and exact portions are not important. The benefits flowing from bone meal are almost unknown, and should be known, by the estimated twenty millions who suffer the pains of arthritis, bursitis, gout, neuritis—even related ailments where the results warrant calling bone meal a miracle longevity food.

From bone meal you may expect the needed calcium supplies for your bones and joints in correct proportions with magnesium and other minerals, for calcium that is not proportioned correctly with other minerals cannot be fully appropriated and utilized by the body. Bone meal is a far better source of calcium than milk ever was; it has been determined that milk, especially when pasteurized, can lead to a porous state of the body's long bones, whereas bone meal always helps—never harms—human bone tissue. Since nearly 100 percent of our skeletal frame is calcium, bone meal, being the richest and most absorbable kind of calcium known, is a miracle item that belongs in the daily diet of every arthritic.

Sunshine: While sunshine is not really a food, it does provide the needed amount of appropriable vitamin D and should be employed daily in your get-well program. Why do sunbaths help arthritics? Through heliotherapy, or exposure to the sun, and by a process of photosynthesis, your body absorbs the D vitamin which aids in mineral utilization, and absorbing the needed minerals is a must in arthritis. About 15 to 30 minutes daily before 10 in the morning and after four in the afternoon is advised as a daily dose of sunshine, exposing all areas of the skin. If entirely private, get on hands and knees and for about three minutes, spread apart the buttocks and allow the sun to reach the anal area; it is a region that never gets sun-exposure and my own researches have shown that when the anus is sunned, the adjacent ganglia benefit and by extension there is neurological profit in the entire organism.

THE HALF DOZEN MIRACLE FOODS FOR ARTHRITIC JOINTS

Cherries appear to have an affinity for gouty and inflamed or rheumatic tissues. When a single food can assuage even the miseries of gout and make the big toes of gout sufferers feel normal in a few days, as cherries have been shown to do, then it can be classed as a kind of miracle food. The ideal way to derive such benefits is to eat about a half pound to one pound of cherries as the sole breakfast item. By eating cherries and only cherries until about two in the afternoon, and then the other raw foods on the program in various amounts and combinations, in less than a month many have reported not only astonishing results in their arthritis but a general upgrading of their entire health, with other ailments that they thought they had to live with also giving way.

Alfalfa is another healing food with astonishing values in ailments of the joints. It was discovered centuries ago by Arab people who dubbed it "Great Father of Foods," in their idiom AL-FAL-FA. It also supplies calcium for sick or undernourished joints, bones, etc. I recommend alfalfa in tablets or powder, about 12 tablets a day or as a tea drunk either warm or cool, whenever a beverage is desired.

Yogurt supplies both a good and quite desirable store of calcium plus the protective lactic acid bacilli which provide intestinal health and keep fungus infections in check. Four ounces of yogurt at bedtime is helpful because at that time it mixes with no other food in the stomach and is fully utilized. Always my preference is for plain yogurt, not the kind that is embroidered with factory-added fruits or sweets of any kind. If desired, add a bit of raw honey, especially if one is sleepless, because this encourages natural sleep. Also one can add one's own fresh fruit, such as a ripe banana or sliced peaches.

Blackstrap Molasses, about one tablespoonful daily, is a miracle food that equals a large steak or several eggs in nutritional value without the harm of any toxemic residues or undesirable after effects. If bowel evacuations reveal black stools, or stools much darker than normal, reduce the amount of blackstrap molasses you ingest because your system may be incapable of absorbing quite all of the rich, energizing, beneficial iron in a full tablespoon of the product, as good as it otherwise is. A single tablespoonful of blackstrap molasses also supplies up to a hefty 50 milligrams of valuable pyridoxine—a matter of unusual importance to arthritis victims.

Asparagus is especially useful if the system is in an overly acid state and needs to be toned down to a lower pH, or more desirable acid levels, meaning a more balanced acid/alkaline state. When eating asparagus many people notice the odor of ammonia in the urine. Ammonia is highly alkaline, the opposite of acid in the system. In the three-month program that I strongly recommend for arthritic cases, I urge the consumption of daily asparagus spears to continue neutralizing the strong acids in the system, then, after the three months, I advise taking canned asparagus spears, fluid and all, in a blenderized frothy whip, as a morning pick-me-up drink that both energizes and deacidifies the body.

Pecans, and indeed all nuts if raw and unsalted, are helpful if taken as the protein items of nutrition by arthritic sufferers, those with rheumatic ills, especially victims of rheumatoid arthritis. I have discovered best results when arthritis patients take up to three ounces of pecans, sometimes mixed with almonds and cashews, always raw and unsalted, for their noontime meal along with merely a raw vegetable salad plate. The salad may have plain yogurt as a dressing. Then, for the other meals of the day I allow no protein items at all, confining the other foods to soups, fruits, grains, salads, cooked vegetables and the like. This program of pecans only for lunch and no protein foods at other times, alone has, I believe, contributed more to the rehabilitation of arthritic cases than any one other technique except that of returning the misaligned body to mechanical adjustment. For non-arthritics, about a dozen pecans daily will sufficiently supply the body's pyridoxine needs.

FINAL RECOMMENDATIONS

There were other recommendations aside from the foregoing list that I gave to Big Mike, and to most other victims of arthritis. Chiefly, they were:

If during the advised three-month period you feel a strong urge for cooked food, you may eat the whites of one or two poached eggs, not the yolks (unless you also have a heart problem), say, about every other day or twice a week. The whites contain an amino acid—also found in peanuts—of special value in your arthritis, tending to nourish arthritic joints.

If the scales show that your body is getting out of balance structurally, or when you stand in front of (or to the side of) the string that you hung from the ceiling you note that you are again getting out of alignment, then in addition to bowling left-handedly you should try doing a lot of Primordial Walks. While alking on hands and feet (not hands and knees) you will ᵤₑgin the process of using the unused and unexercised muscles and tendons, ligaments, cartilages that need a workout to set you right. It will benefit you doubly to do the Primordial Walk with bare feet on the good earth, such as a grassy lawn, thus absorbing the emanations of the soil and not insulating yourself from the earth by way of shoes or sneakers.

The Primordial Walk was first introduced by this writer in another book published by Parker Publishing Company, *Doctor Morrison's Miracle Body Tune-Up for Rejuvenated Health,* and later expanded in another Parker book, *Doctor Morrison's Miracle Guide to Pain-Free Health and Longevity,* and it is one of the few exercises that may be attempted even by debilitated and elderly people, just a few steps at the start within one's capacity to do. In unbelievably short time the improvement in energy from the Primordial Walk enables even the very sick and old to increase the time and energy expended in this effort. Besides, if so rushed that you simply cannot find time for other important body-aligning drills, doing only the Primordial Walk will, in many cases, give the various parts of your body just about all the exercise they need.

To optimize your health you must avoid sugar in all forms. *Even a few teaspoonsful can upset the calcium-phosphorus balance within your body.* Such upsets can lead to increased arthritic pains, pyorrhea and tooth decay. Accordingly, do not be lulled by the hyperbolic TV ads that sing the praises of "pure cane sugar" for it is, I have found, pure poison for arthritis sufferers.

White flour in all forms does just about the same harm done by white refined sugar, and even brown sugar to some extent. The one sure, fool-proof safety zone for arthritic people is to think of the bakery with its customary baked goods (out of white flour) as "The Poisoneria" rather than The Bakery. If you think me too severe in this—and I am entirely objective in this value judgment—merely try eating some bakery cake or donuts at bedtime and note the increased pains the following morning.

To further optimize your health on a very positive note, take daily without fail from 400 to 800 International Units of vitamin E, vitamin D from sunbaths supplemented by an occasional vitamin D tablet or capsule, as much as two grams of vitamin C (which is 2,000 milligrams), preferably from rose hips or acerola berries, and plenty of yeast for its B vitamins—about two to four teaspoonsful of the powder or the equivalent in tablets. Do not fear overdoing the bone meal tablets or powder; your system uses what calcium it needs and throws off through the urinary apparatus whatever it rejects, and with no harm to you.

You must stop taking aspirin or other salycilates. *They reduce your body's ability to absorb the iron you need for energy and healing.* In cases under study, after salicylates such as aspirin, Anacin, Bufferin and the like were *withdrawn,* iron absorption rose from 30 to a whopping 80 percent.

RESULTS

After only a month with us in California, Big Mike felt unbelievably better and prepared to return to his home in Texas. Our parting was a memorable scene. The big fellow went over all of the foregoing with me and then said to me in an emotionally charged voice:

"Good God, Doctor, this here's the equivalent of three or four university courses in getting and keeping health, or equal to reading a thousand books by the most expensive specialists. It's *life-information*—that's what it is. I can't think of enough words to thank you."

He followed the program exactly for another two months, reporting by phone that in less than another month he had lost all pains, that no trick knees or tennis elbows or joint discomforts reared their ugly heads anymore. He was continuing with a half pound of cherries for breakfast, nothing more. For lunch he consumed barely anything more than a huge plate of raw salad vegetables, using plain yogurt, with or without lemon juice, as a dressing. Then his foods were chosen from among raw nuts for protein needs, uncooked corn on the cob (which he declared unexpectedly delicious), papaya, tomatoes, squash, mushrooms, steamed cauliflower (and sometimes even raw), carrots and cabbage and lots of carrot juice drunk daily. At bedtime he developed the new good habit of eating a four-ounce cup of plain yogurt, sometimes with a banana if hungry, and this helped him sleep "like a babe." He claimed it also made his digestion so good that, said he, "I want to bust with joy."

I was of course very gratified with the man's results, and with his exuberant desire to share it all with me. I complimented him on his self-discipline, also on his desire to tell others about the newly-found road to health.

"Eating this way is no sacrifice at all," he declared over the phone. "Not when it makes me feel so good that every day is a month of first-class Sundays."

Miss Edwina was a middle-aged artist who had never married because, as she put it, "painting is my life and I'm wedded to my art." She was gifted with great talent but since developing some years earlier a crippling of the hands, her fingers were gnarled and she could barely hold brushes in her hands. *"Ni modo,"* she said in Spanish, smiling through her tears, for Edwina was also a linguist, "if eventually brushes have to be strapped to my hands that's no more than happened to such masters as Manet, Cézanne and Renoir." She opened and closed her fingers with some effort, contemplating them philosophically. "Perhaps it's because we have to grip our brushes so hard and long that crippled hands become an artist's syndrome," she said.

The brave lady's case had been variously diagnosed as osteoarthritis, arthritis deformans, infectious arthritis, even just brachial and manual neuritis. But one thing was so evident that it needed no diagnostic confirmation: the swollen, deformed state of her fingers and knuckle joints. Aside from this, Edwina was about 30 pounds overweight. To complicate matters further she was a lifelong dedicated vegetarian who eschewed flesh food and would not take bone meal (derived from animals) no matter how much help this item offered, so other means of getting utilizable calcium into the lady had to be employed, sometimes circuitously. But she was brave withal—a truly brave and very helpful lady in the most intelligent way possible.

On examination, I found in her spine between her shoulder blades a scoliosis, or S-shaped double curvature. This pinched off the nerves that fed nutrition and energy *and functional direction* to the poor woman's arms and chest cage, which accounted for both the brachial neuritis and intercostal pains, the constant distress in her ribs. On top of this she had an old problem of cysts in her ovaries, and when cysts are present in either ovaries or the uterus I suggest, along with plenty of bioflavonoid drinks, a full week or longer without eating any protein foods at all. This forces the body to consume its own uneliminated protein accumulations (which at base cysts are), and thus the cystic contents are often eaten up *naturally,* for the body needs daily protein and if not provided by food intake it will consume resident piled-up accumulations of protein consistency.

When I recounted to the talented Edwina the complexity of her problems—the gnarled hands plus the obesity plus the ovarian cysts—and commiserated that for all that she had talents not given to the commonalty, she said to me thoughtfully, "The Lord giveth and the Lord taketh away . . . blessed be the Name of the Lord." How could I discount the purity of such faith? When she saw on the two bathroom scales how far off center she was, and when the plumbline revealed how badly she measured out of adjustment, she raced into the simple realigning exercises like one reborn and lo! her lopsidedness gave way with unexpected ease to two simple drills. Several times a day while lying on the floor she drew both knees to her chest and laced her fingers as best she could manage over her knees, hugging herself tightly into a little basket, then rolled from side to side until tired. This basket position was an activity which loosened the lateral ligaments of her spine and began letting her double curvature give way. When the dear woman saw on the two scales how very much more nearly even this simple exercise made her she pursued her basket roll as many as 20 times a day, whenever she took a break from her easel.

The other drill that worked well with Edwina was the Sway-and-Arch that I had written about in other books and magazine pieces; it consisted merely of being on hands and knees and alternately dipping the spine down as far as possible, then arching it up as far as it could go. By doing this until somewhat tired and concentrating on both the areas between the shoulders and the lower spine, the tendency is for the whole spine to come into correct vertebral juxtaposition—which was what happened in Edwina's case.

In lieu of bone meal, which the lady ruled out because of deepfelt vegetarian principles, I recommended an extra daily spoonful of blackstrap molasses and also sunflower seeds as her daily protein intake for a month or two. The molasses contained the next best source of utilizable calcium for her arthritic needs.

In the matter of the morning ration of cherries as her sole breakfast food, I restricted her to half a pound, for she was overweight and the fruit sugar in cherries alone would prevent the desired weight loss.

One thing that the lady came to understand clearly was this. Those with joint pains and aching bodies who went on a program of bone meal, or a good calcium substitute, together with black-strap molasses, and also ate a daily ration of cherries, yogurt and the other miracle foods, hardly ever failed to achieve rewarding results. By this is meant a decided diminution or even complete cessation of their bodily pains. All this, of course, provided they took the trouble to place their distorted bodies, if misaligned, back into mechanical adjustment so that the system could absorb and utilize the miracle food values in their healing items of nutrition.

Later, when it proved that two daily tablespoonsful of blackstrap molasses brought on unwanted symptoms by way of blackish stools, I advised reducing or changing the intake to one tablespoonful during the day and the other at bedtime when it interfered with no other food in the stomach. This put into her system one tablespoonful of molasses around the clock, spaced about twelve hours apart, and it happily solved the difficulty. I recommend trying this as a physiologically acceptable technique if blackstrap molasses deliver to the system too much iron for easy absorption, as shown by dark stools.

In order to make it ineradicable in Edwina's brain that even the best food is only *potentially* valuable, and not *actually* beneficial until it reaches the cells and is utilized by the body, and that a body that is out of structural adjustment cannot properly utilize even the finest potentially good nutrients, I gave her a kind of Principles and Practice sheet that eventually became a Philosophy Paper for all arthritic patients. Here is what the paper said.

FOR ARTHRITIS PATIENTS . . . READ AND HEED

Why I Do What I Do

I do not ask you to believe what follows but only to read and consider this thoughtfully. The author (your doctor) has long had the theory that many forms of arthritis stem from bad mechanical or structural balance in the human vertical straight-up-and-down (as opposed to the four-footed animal's horizontal) body. Why so? Because, based on seeing several thousand cases, a structurally distorted body cannot absorb and utilize the needed healing nutrients out of the foods you consume any more than a machine that is out of adjustment can be expected to work right. It is gospel truth that the potential value is not a food's actual value. If structural distortions interfere with nutritional utilization, it is as though the person had not eaten any good food of nutritional value. So the body must be in alignment, proper adjustment, or mechanical balance, *as a machine,* or it cannot do the job of utilizing healing food nutrients.

Saying it another way, much arthritis (perhaps all, to some extent) comes from having the different bodily parts jarred or jolted mechanically out of position by the various falls and jolts and jarring impacts we sustain in the course of living—even the falls we endure when first learning to walk as vertical creatures—any of which can rattle or strain spinal bones and other parts of the body out of their correct mechanical position. All of this usually causes the malpositioned parts, especially the vertebrae, to pinch off nerves. Nerve pressures interfere with the flow of impulses to the digestive organs and other organs, which is like a motor that is not properly plugged in to the source of its "juice." When organs suffer from an improper flow of impulses due to nerve pressures, the body's resistance is lowered and there can ensue a piling-up of concretions and calcium deposits in the various joints, including the formation of ankylosing spicules that dig painfully into the tissues. This is arthritis. So I set about devising ways to return the mechanically distorted body back into correct alignment, hoping thus to remove the cause of arthritis.

Proving the abovementioned theory was no easy matter. But after several false research starts and many different attempts, quite a simple way was discovered. It consisted of measuring the body's misalignments or mechanical distortions by the two easy devices already taught to you: weighing yourself before and after any activity on two bathroom scales, and noting how you line up while standing in front of a vertical string, also sideways to the vertical string. If your favorite exercise or sport or calisthenic drill showed immediately afterward that you weighed out more nearly in balance and that you lined up "more true," then it was right for you and should be pursued; but if the activity was wrong it would show a greater imbalance and greater offsidedness as measured by the string, and it should be abandoned. Thus you had criteria or guidelines by which you could, all by yourself, make the determinations and bypass the doctors—most of whom do not know these things anyway.

Now the surprise finding. People with arthritis (any kind, all kinds, it appeared) who were grossly lopsided on the scales and imbalanced at the string and then did corrective breathing exercises such as the diaphragmatic drill, or played tennis with the left hand, or did a few rounds of the Primordial Walk or whatever else that returned them to a more equal weight distribution, *lost their arthritic symptoms.* Their symptoms disappeared in almost exact ratio to their loss of misalignments. It proved that mechanical distortions bring on arthritic ailments and that mechanical corrections eliminate the symptoms of arthritis. I do not ask anyone to believe this, only to try it for a week or two and see. In no way can such a test possibly harm you. And it may very well benefit you enormously in the most easy and painless way imaginable.

TWO PERFECT ROADS TO SELF-EVALUATION

Now comes the real prize, the icing on the cake. *Just about the same thing works when you are on raw foods for a week or two.* That is, the pains and symptoms of arthritis subside, sometimes magically vanish, evaporate as though they'd never been. Let us say the scales showed you twenty pounds heavier on one side than on the other. You do the drills and exercises that work *for you,* those that bring you into mechanical balance as seen on the scales or at the plumb-bob string) and you lose your arthritic pains in tune with your weight loss and return to mechanical alignment. That's one way. Now, let's say you have this twenty-pound difference in the weight of each half of the body, and the string shows you lopsided with low shoulder, high hip, inability to turn the head as far one way as the other, etc., and instead of the exercises you go on an exclusive program of raw foods for two weeks. What happens? Why, miracle of miracles, the arthritic symptoms disappear as they did under the other (exercising) program.

Raw foods will improve elimination. Usually they bring about a desirable weight loss in obesity. In ways not yet clearly understood both weight loss and better elimination mean an end to the pile-up of calcium and other deposits that create arthritic miseries. Experiments in research projects have shown that *you can induce arthritis in animals by feeding them solely cooked foods.* As shown in the Gerson Cancer Cure, raw foods increase the oxygenating capacity of all bodily cells because raw plant life in the human body stimulates cellular activity, or metabolic function, through the electric quality in the living raw foodstuff.

Also a daily sunbath during this raw food program provides vitamin D through the skin and it is vitamin D that aids in mineral utilization, which is a must in arthritis.

Besides a daily heaping plate of raw salad vegetables, the one- or two-week experimental program on raw foods should include, in addition to bone meal and the half dozen miracle longevity foods for arthritis, such helping items as raw (peeled) apples, a devotion to which will give up the valuable pectin for intestinal health, apricots and other fruits for their carbohydrate nutrition, strawberries because of their natural content of pain-stilling salicylates, and grapes for quick energy needs.

So there are, experimentally, two natural and easy (and beautifully safe) roads to cleaning arthritis out of the human organism: the exercise way that brings the misaligned body into mechanical rightness and the exclusive raw food program that upgrades elimination while vitalizing the tissues. But, now, what is the obvious lesson here? It should be clear to any serious healthseeker that the way to win the whole ball game is to *devote a trial week or two to both avenues.* Test yourself on the scales and string and do the physical drills that put you back into mechanical adjustment as a machine. At the same time also devote a week or two to eating only raw rejuvenating foods. Just devote a fortnight out of your life to this two-pronged way to health and see if you ever again have any desire to suffer arthritic tortures or take drugs for such tortures.

In our lady painter's case one further activity was added to her program. It was needed because she suffered intercostal pains, a kind of neuritis in the rib cage that made breathing distressful. I call this activity the Dowager's Hump, as have others before me, because it is a drill for all who desire better breathing room in the chest and wish to overcome a round-shouldered state that doctors call kyphosis. This is done by clasping both palms behind your back at about the region of the hips and rolling the elbows inwards as hard and as far as you can. If necessary, lace the fingers together to keep both palms touching or tightly glued to each other. The action of rolling in the elbows raises the chest and at the same time straightens the spine in the area of the shoulder blades—a godsend drill for those with spinal curvatures in this region of the spinal column. Edwina was specifically ordered to do the Dowager's Hump drill several times a day, but most especially at night just before retiring.

"Why at bedtime?" she asked.

"Because of this very correct reason," I explained. "By enlarging your chest cage just before turning in for the night you provide your chest with more breathing space during the hours of sleep. This means more and better oxygenation during the night, and oxygen is the staff of life. But, besides this, I'd like you to remember a firm rule that doctors ought to spread around the world. *What you gain at bedtime you tend to retain during bedtime.* It is during sleep that your body repairs its damages, not while you are traipsing around throughout the rush-rush hours. So when you provide yourself advantages by way of breathing drills or miracle foods to take you through the night, you thereby give yourself great healthifying advantages also."

Moreover, because Edwina was given to taking sauna baths (which had once temporarily reduced her arthritic pains), the matter was explained to this intelligent lady in terms she never forgot.

"Sauna baths promote artificial sweating, Edwina. What is *artificial* is not likely to produce *natural* health. For sweating to be natural it must be induced by working the body into a perspiring level, such as being active in a garden under the sun. Artificial sweating is not really good for anyone in the long run, because nature desires only a cleansing wash through the millions of pores in the body by way of an induced activity. However, with your kind of gnarled fingers that indicate an overly acid state, I can recommend two kinds of baths to fit your needs and alkalize the body."

EASY WAY TO NEUTRALIZE BODY ACIDS

I advised her to immerse herself in a tub of water that was just about as hot as the inner temperature of her body—98 or 99 degrees, give or take a degree, which she could determine by dropping a thermometer into the water or hanging one over the side of the tub. This could be called a "neutral bath" because the water ouside the body just about equalled the temperature inside the body itself. Under such conditions, with the entire body framework and musculature suspended between equivalent temperatures, all the organs and tissues and everything else in the body that possibly could relax and let go, do relax and let go. The tense muscles and spastic areas and contracted regions enveloped by one's skin all tend to give way while hanging or immersed between neutral temperatures outside and inside the body.

Edwina understood this and was enchanted by the technique. She saw that such energy as one normally gives up, quite unwittingly, in fighting tensions and spasms, could by "neutral bathing" be saved for healing the damages inside the body. With the exception of the twice-weekly alkalizing baths, hot ones, that I advised in order to quickly rid her body of the highly acid state, this neutral bath was her nightly bathing recommendation.

This alkalizing bath to lower a high systemic acid level was a technique I had experimented with in connection with a quite different syndrome some years earlier, and it was unbelievably easy to do. One merely filled a bathtub with water as hot as could be comfortably borne. Before immersion into the tub up to the neck for about 15 minutes, a cup of hot water was prepared with a half teaspoonful of bicarbonate of soda stirred into it. After lowering oneself into the tub the water and bicarbonate was sipped slowly, which usually brought volumes of perspiration from the pores as it alkalized the overly acid system.

The droplets of sweat that poured out of one in this bath were customarily sour to the smell, indicating a washing out of acid toxic wastes from the body. After finishing the drink Edwina was told to sink her distorted fingers entirely under water for the remaining 15 minutes of the bath. Within two weeks of this program, taking only four or five of these baths along with the other vital raw foods and exercises, the lady reported more mobility in her hands and was able to flex formerly inflexible fingers. Now she was advised that after drinking the bicarbonate to neutralize her acid state and immersing her fingers into the hot water of this twice-weekly bath, she was to have a sponge rubber ball in each hand and work her fingers further under the water, squeezing and relaxing the ball in rhythmic movements. The knobby and bony protuberances on her hands were of course, irreversible, but within three months this advanced case of arthritis regained almost full and normal use of hands and fingers and could carry on with not even a twinge of pain.

"Think of it," she said with great emotion. "After years of this infernal arthritis I can now, in just three months, move my fingers without pain. It is something not to be believed."

"But some of this may return," I warned her. "If you keep on with your sedentary life, sitting all day hunched over a drawing board or canvas, your body may again lapse into mechanical misalignment so you must keep on with the exercises along with the program of eating the miracle healing foods." Then I leaned into her and made an emphatic point. "The conditions that caused your trouble the first time will, if repeated, probably cause it again."

She ruminated over this for a long moment. Then she asked an extraordinarily intelligent question.

"Tell me, please," she said quietly. "If you say that even the best food cannot be utilized properly when the body is mechanically out of adjustment, how can you also say that *either* the exercise way that aligns the body *or* the miracle eating way can produce results in a week or two, as an experiment? I'd think that if you don't attend to bringing the body back into alignment, the foods alone wouldn't do it."

Remarkable lady, this one. She had bored into the question like a logician and scientist.

"It does seem odd, doesn't it?" I admitted. "But both courses do work *to a degree.* It's like the distorted vegetarian full of nerve pressures who does nothing to realign his body but does drive away his pains by sticking to live raw foods alone. What happens is this. By consuming only cleansing foods that are vital and non-irritating, he creates in the body *an internal environment so clean and toxin-free* that even with nerve pressures he can enjoy a modicum of health and a state of pain-free existence. But it is a precarious state of health so long as nerve pressures also exist and remain uncorrected. How can this be proved? I have seen it proved many times. These people with bodies out of adjustment but with almost perfect eating habits have created in their body an internal environment so mild and poison-free and easy for the organs to operate in that, even with nerve-pressure interferences, they can enjoy a certain state of health. But let them violate even a little bit—wow! Let them so much as eat one sweet roll or have a slab of butter or a soft drink—then see them hawking up mucus and suffering the symptoms of a cold the next day. The level of health attainable through foods alone (while the body is mechanically out of adjustment) is just not stable enough to be desired."

Edwina went over the little speech with me point by point. At last she understood it; it was sophisticated doctoring talk to fire at a lay person.

"Well, now I am doubly sure," she said with conviction. "Both roads are for me. I promise you to do the physical drills for my mechanical body and the eating program for my disgestive side. Have I got it right, Doctor?"

"You are merely wonderful," I said. And she was.

SUMMARY

Principal food: BONE MEAL

Assisting miracle foods: CHERRIES
                            ASPARAGUS
                            YOGURT
                            ALFALFA
                            RAW PECANS

Secondary healing foods: BLACKSTRAP MOLASSES
                            STRAWBERRIES
                            CARROT JUICE
                            PEANUTS
                            EGG WHITES
                            SWEET POTATO
                            PAPAYA
                            WATERMELON
                            PEARS
                            MELONS
                            TOMATOES
                            PEACHES
                            HONEY (raw, in small amounts)
                            YEAST (2 to 4 teaspoons)
                            VITAMIN E (400 to 800 I.U.s daily)
                            VITAMIN C (2 grams daily)
                            VITAMIN D (sun plus capsules)

12

Common Foods
With Uncommon Power
to Restore Skin and Hair

The skin is an organ. It is the body's largest organ. It envelopes all other organs like a tight wraparound. It weighs about six pounds and has a million breathing vents called pores.

Biologically, the human hair, and even fingernails, are extensions of the human skin; therefore I treat them here in the same section.

People actually *suffer* most from ailments of the internal viscera, but over a span of fifty professional years I've learned that they are concerned most about the skin. Its appearance. Taking pride in its glow of health—or suffering profoundly when it is sallow, lifeless and ugly.

I have often written in books and articles that the health of the skin is not the result of what you put on but of what you put in. But lately, as a clean-minded person, I have changed my mind. What one puts inside the body is in truth and fact what will eventually show on the skin as healthfulness, or the lack thereof. Late researches, however, have shown me that a few miracle food items such as wheat germ oil and lecithin and yogurt rubbed onto the skin, as will be discussed presently, do indeed make for health by way of disappearing burn marks and arteriole blotches, by ironing out wrinkles, and suchlike.

The more recent investigations and controlled projects

have also revealed a rather remarkable new aspect to this dermatological business. Would you believe that at times bad skin is in fact a sign that the underlying organs are in reasonably good health? How so? Because it is now understood that often the skin takes up the burden of discharging bodily wastes (by way of pustules, pimples, etc.) and thus diverts the disease process from the intestines or liver, for example.

I am still of the opinion that the healing foods which I shall discuss directly are healing and healthifying items for the skin as specifically as raw wheat germ with its built-in anti-clotting d-alpha tocopherol is a food for the heart. But now I am equally sure of another thing. Raw potato slices and parsnips and egg-and-lemon and others I wish to talk about have great and exciting uses *as rub-ons* for blemished and itching and wrinkled skin.

WHEAT GERM OIL RANKS FIRST

First, which food can exactly and specifically be called a miracle food for the skin in the context of feeding and beautifying the skin from the inside rather than rubbing it on from the outside? There are several, really. But the one great item of skin nutrition that in my opinion tends to restore the health and appearance of the human epidermis is wheat germ oil. Let me explain.

Wheat germ oil contains inositol. Inositol seems to be a kind of hair-food; it often stops falling hair and reverses baldness when taking pantothenic acid in the form of brewer's yeast. Also inositol serves this important purpose: it improves the body's fat metabolism and thus takes this burden away from the skin.

Until the age of 35 Mrs. Frances was an attractive upper middle class wife and mother with good mental ballast and buoyant physical health. Then her husband fell into a bad investment and suffered financial reverses, after which he attempted suicide. Soon thereafter Mrs. Frances developed a case of eczema which in time subsided only to reappear as exfoliative dermatitis.

When she came to see me five years later, large areas of the lady's body presented skin inflammation that resulted in shedding of dry, ugly, scaly flakes. Since the skin problem followed the emotional trauma of her husband's attempted suicide, it was thought to be a case for psychoanalysts or psychiatrists. For five years she had given herself over to many in these fields, but none had yielded any help or diminution of the dry, red, ugly, brownish scales. Coming to me was a genuine last resort.

From past experience I was almost sure this was somehow tied up with a digestive insufficiency; I reasoned that if her evacuations were truly complete the skin would not have been called upon to eliminate whatever poisons were forming in her body. Also, such inflammatory skin conditions had responded in the past to DNA- and RNA-bearing foods along with the well-researched amazing healing foods for the skin.

When she was instructed to apply wheat germ oil liberally to the inflamed areas, the copious desquamation or shedding of the surface skin cells lessened within a single week. Along with the amazing healing foods, which I now used in all skin cases as given at the end of this chapter, I concentrated on nucleic acid foods such as nuts, sardines, spinach, oatmeal, bran (rather heavily for better roughage and intestinal elimination), peas and pinto beans and the dark meat of chicken. All these were rich in DNA (deoxyribonucleic acid), which kind of packages our inherited potentials and RNA (ribonucleic acid), which renews our body cells under the direction of DNA.

Mrs. Frances burst in on me less than a month later with, "Doctor, will you look at this skin." She extended her forearm which had been particularly red and dry. It was smooth and normal in color. She pulled down her V-neck and her chest or sternal area was equally smooth and healthy. "I've gone into playing racquetball," she said. "Before every game I lather myself well with wheat germ oil, then leave it on for another half hour after each game before I shower the stuff away. Is it that that does the work?"

It was the entire program that made Mrs. Frances well in an amazingly short period, less than two months. It demonstrated the body's capacity to return to normal quickly when the skin was fed externally with highly nutritional wheat germ oil, and then—most importantly—fed internally by such amazing healing foods as wheat germ, lecithin, yeast and yogurt and blackstrap molasses and barley water, besides the foods rich in DNA and RNA as listed above.

I learned a very important lesson from this case of Mrs. Frances. She happened to like dry cereals and was fairly crazy about the taste of yogurt. Consequently, with my enthusiastic approval she made a daily dish of wheat germ with yogurt instead of milk, mushing them both around and then adding a tablespoon of blackstrap molasses for taste and a few spoonfuls of lecithin flakes. This so perfectly suited her taste that she had this as a noonday dish also, then even ate the mixture as a between-meals snack. I was alert to the implications of this and to its potentials, so I began advising this four-food dish to other people with skin or hair (and even nerve-related) problems. Every last one responded better than formerly. I learned that a doctor must learn from his patients. A dish of wheat germ/yogurt/blackstrap molasses/lecithin was what later helped many patients because I'd learned of its value from Mrs. Frances.

Wheat germ oil is also a rich source of pyridoxine. This works in the body to increase peristaltic action. Such intestinal activity, of course, results in better food absorption and therefore less skin blemishes that follow in the wake of poor digestion. (Pecans also contain pyridoxine, making it a fine food for human nerves.) But beyond all this, wheat germ oil, as distinguished from the wheat germ cereal, is a direct, local, rub-on skin food without peer.

Rub wheat germ oil into the skin and leave it on overnight, then see what happens. Smear it over burned skin and see how quickly the burn heals. Spread it, along with liquid lecithin obtainable in any health food store, over leg areas where varicose veins bulge unattractively, or where tiny red arterioles show in the skin, and in so many happy cases it appears to feed the area *directly,* with observably improved appearance in a few weeks.

What about wrinkles? Take a teaspoonful of wheat germ oil every day internally, and do so if you can manage along with a tablespoonful of liquid lecithin, and at the same time smear both the wheat germ oil and liquid lecithin over the wrinkled areas— then note how the wrinkles tend to smooth out. In many cases it is really nothing short of amazing, which may in large part be due to combining the wheat germ oil with lecithin because the latter is an integral part of every cell of the body, including skin cells.

Now do an experiment that I have done with success many times, combining wheat germ oil with plain yogurt. Rub a mixture of both deeply into your facial blemishes or outbreaks; leave it on overnight; awake one morning, perhaps a week later, to a most rewarding result.

Besides its quite exciting uses in cases of deep skin wrinkles, wheat germ oil is a precious find in warts and skin tags. I have with great satisfaction advised this oil as a rub-on substance in neoplasms, assorted skin growths, pedunculated tags, heavy warts and especially in silver-scaled psoriasis on elbows, knees, etc. Some have reported unbelievable results. None has ever reported any harmful effects.

Some who took seriously and followed closely the recommendation to use wheat germ oil both inside and on the outer skin, and in particular those who consumed liquid lecithin at the same time, boasted about the reversal of baldness, while nearly all reported much improved digestion.

Charlie was a middle-aged gas station owner with an almost pathological concern about a bald spot the size of a half dollar near the front left hairline.

One year earlier he had risen swiftly while working under a car and banged his head severely right at the spot where he thereafter became bald. The dermatological experts had diagnosed it as alopecia neurotica, which only means nerve-induced baldness. When I explained this to Charlie he exploded. "Dammit, I paid good money to be told in Latin what they could have said in plain English. Sure I hurt the nerves there, that's why my hair doesn't grow on that spot—but what can they do about it?"

Since the condition was one connected with nerve damage, I put the anxious man who was so extraordinarily bashful about his bald spot on foods with amazing healing power for the nervous system. He ate regularly and plentifully such foods as pecans, soybeans, brewer's yeast and wheat germ, and he drank copiously of alfalfa tea, rice water and barley water—but only with moderate success. He thought he saw a thin sprouting of hair on the bald spot, but it proved a false alarm. Then I asked him to rub with speed and vigor raw wheat germ oil directly onto the bald area, and by doing this nightly and then covering it overnight with a skull cap a few fine hairs began to show. This, however, was not enough to please either him or me. The case required a more definitive program.

I recommended a twice-daily sunbath of 20 minutes, exposing the bald area onto which wheat germ oil had been applied, doing this at, say, 10 a.m. and 4 p.m. before the sun's rays were so direct and hot as to do harm. In addition to the nerve-feeding foods, Charlie now ate regularly those amazing healing foods for the skin and hair: raw garlic, brown rice, sunflower seeds, pumpkin seeds, blackstrap molasses. In two weeks the hairs began to show black and visible. Between times he rubbed onto the bald spot raw cucumber slices, raw potato slices, slices of parsnip and even okra and fresh lemon slices. At night, before applying wheat germ oil for his hours in bed, Charlie made a hair wash solution of warm water with black pepper dissolved in it, rinsing and drying his hair thoroughly. That did it. Every day he came by the office on the way to his station, not for a professional visit but just to show me the new crop of sprouting hair since the day before. "Golly!" he exulted. "Ten weeks ago I was bald and today I am a man." He bent forward to reveal the bald half-dollar spot now covered with a dark fuzz. It was indeed true that his alopecia neurotica had changed to alopecia no mas exista.

HELPS SHORTNESS OF BREATH

In our society, living in our kind of polluted atmosphere, everyone needs a better oxygen supply. A single teaspoonful of wheat germ oil can enable one to "make do" with a lesser amount of good oxygen—or, put another way, make much better use of what poor oxygen is available. It has been held that even so small an intake as one teaspoonful of wheat germ oil is equivalent to placing oneself under an oxygen tent. Thus, those with asthma or emphysema along with their skin problems reported the most gratifying results from the wheat germ oil/lecithin therapy.

For shortness of breath, the wheat germ oil approach was an unexpected gift of health without side effects of any kind. For poor blood flow to the skin, this oil approach was the quickest, safest, sanest answer. So after viewing the findings I had the following little speech for people with skin ailments.

"If you wisely consume some wheat germ oil daily, and

additionally rub both wheat germ oil and liquid lecithin onto the unattractive or sick skin areas, and at the same time enrich your insides with brown rice, pumpkin seeds, sunflower seeds, black-strap molasses and brewer's yeast—ah, then you will be purchasing the finest and most dependable health-and-life insurance available anywhere. It'll be mental and emotional besides physical health, for having a skin that you and others will love to see can supply mental and emotional nourishment of the first rate. And this will be trouble-free health that you will gain this "food-way," for from this route there are never the iatrogenic or pesky side-effect diseases to deal with afterward, as is the case with the drug route."

An unexpected reward flowing from the use of wheat germ oil and the other amazing healing foods for the skin was in the department of energy. People lost their tiredness, their mid-morning lassitude, their customary afternoon dreariness. What happened was that the wheat germ oil enabled more oxygen to reach their cells, including of course, skin cells, and as the muscle tissue became oxygenated/energized it expelled the strain of tiredness that showed up in body and skin tone.

Now some peripheral items, some additional helping items, and also some no-no items.

Coffee revealed some surprising effects. More than in other tests, coffee in connection with wheat germ oil appeared to wipe out the expected benefits. It gave cause to wonder. Perhaps it was because coffee sometimes developed an inositol deficiency, I'm not sure. But when the results we looked for were not forthcoming and on inquiry I learned that the patients were taking coffee, by ordering them to quit the beverage the wheat germ oil, in most cases, began to show the anticipated magic.

ADDITIONAL MIRACLE FOODS

Curiously, raw garlic proved to be another healing food when alopecia areata, or patches of baldness, was the problem. It helped also in ordinary baldness; that is, where the galea, which is a membranous muscle under the top of the head which binds together the forehead muscle and the occipital (back of the head) muscle, needed to be nourished. What one did in addition to swallowing about one clove of chopped garlic daily was rub the raw garlic right onto, and rather deeply into, the bald area.

When the scalp itched we found another helpful technique. Merely a solution of black pepper rubbed into the scalp, allowed to remain an hour and then washed away, relieved both the itch and cleansed the scalp of dandruff. What we found worked best was a level teaspoonful of black pepper boiled in a pint of water, then applied when cooled down to tolerated degree.

If the black pepper failed to help as much as desired, and when we dealt with plain scalp itch uncomplicated by dandruff, rubbing some slices of freshly cut lemon onto the scalp brought the best results.

Many times such simple aids as rubbing raw cucumber slices onto the skin produced rather amazing results. When patients said they saw no results from the cucumber slices, I asked them to try rubbing raw slices of newly cut potato, and this appeared to help in some cases of skin blotches and pigment spots. One Irish lady whose family in the old country knew about dependence upon potatoes declared "Who would think there was also a great medical use for our Irish potatoes!"

Barley water has come to be almost a must in skin cases, a dependably desirable drink for improved skin tone. The British Royal Family has many times declared that its members owe their excellent skin freshness to the daily consumption of barley water. In a recent book about the royal personages, *To Set Before the Queen*, the author wrote that this is a daily drink at every meal, unfailingly. To make barley water, boil one cup of whole barley in about six cups of water for 15 minutes, then drain off the water before it cools. Let it stand until perfectly cool and keep it refrigerated until taken out at mealtimes for use. Since I do not approve of thinning down the digestive enzymes by drinking with meals, barley water can serve as almost the ideal between-meals drink in skin cases.

Some workers in this research field have found okra to be a skin softener (emollient) when rubbed in its raw state on local areas of the skin. Okra is to some offensively sticky. This very quality is useful in cases of heavy crowfeet lines at the eyes or at mouth corners, for when I advised rubbing in the okra before retiring many reported that upon lifting off the okra film the following morning, the wrinkles and lines were less noticeable.

Brittle and unattractively ridged fingernails often profit from the daily use of wheat germ cereal and, as a favored warm beverage, alfalfa tea. Both are rich sources of silicon, a mineral that is naturally health-building for human hair and nails. In some cases fingernails strengthened rather remarkably when raw parsnips were rubbed into them at night, then left on overnight and washed off with cooled-down alfalfa tea in the morning.

REMEMBER TO REMEMBER WHEAT GERM OIL

In our world we live constantly with two strikes against us. As up-and-down bipeds we live against gravity, a fact that causes our blood and other fluids to fight their way uneasily in a straight uphill flow—this is a drag on the circulatory system (strike one). We live in a polluted atmosphere of substandard ecological conditions where we must breathe in contaminants with every breath, which is a drag on our respiratory system (strike two). To offset and balance out these factors I urge the daily consumption of one teaspoonful of wheat germ oil.

For one's health's sake, including one's skin's sake, it is well to remember that wheat germ enables us to carry on, or "make do," with what oxygen supply is available to us. At the same time it also supplies a better *quality* of oxygen to all tissues, by which provision it makes adapting to our substandard ecology more nearly possible. With the skin-nourishing blood needing to be pumped to the face and neck straight uphill (counter-gravitationally), this better flow of oxygen induced by wheat germ oil makes for more attractive skin tone all by itself.

Now, a wee "cop-out" for those who cannot or will not take wheat germ oil along with liquid lecithin, which latter can be a bit of a trial. I give it here rather reluctantly, hoping that readers will take the ideal course rather than the easy one to better health.

The cereal wheat germ itself, purchasable at most supermarkets and all health food stores, contains a quantity of the wheat germ oil. Thus by taking on the good habit of eating wheat germ cereal daily, we will be consuming the wheat germ oil to some degree also. Since we can become enslaved to good habits as easily as to bad ones, I urge the taking on of this new habit: soybean spread in place of butter or margarine. Soybeans are the source of lecithin. By cooking soybeans over a low flame and then mashing them in a blender you can make a paste-like spread that works on bread or toast just like butter. Then, by spreading mashed soybeans on wheat germ bread or toast—well, you thereby consume both lecithin and wheat germ oil, the lecithin resident in the soybeans and the oil in the wheat germ of the bread.

One thing is evident, however. If you do *both,* you win both ways. So I strongly advise taking your daily teaspoonful of wheat germ oil plus the daily tablespoonful of liquid lecithin. Then, as an extra gift to health and beauty, a daily morning cereal of wheat germ with skim milk plus some wheat germ bread or toast that is spread with that delicious mashed soybean substance.

SUMMARY

Principal food for skin and hair: WHEAT GERM OIL

Assisting miracle foods: WHEAT GERM (as a cereal)
LECITHIN (soybeans and liquid lecithin)
YOGURT
BREWER'S YEAST
PECANS (raw, unsalted)
BARLEY WATER
GARLIC
ALFALFA TEA (for silicon)
BLACKSTRAP MOLASSES
SUNFLOWER SEEDS
PUMPKIN SEEDS.
BROWN RICE
RAW CUCUMBERS (rub externally)
RAW POTATO SLICES (externally)
PARSNIPS (externally)
OKRA (externally)
FRESH LEMON (externally)
BLACK PEPPER SOLUTION
EGG-AND-LEMON (hair wash)

13

Foods That Can Often Regenerate Damaged Nerves

Until recently it has been widely held that nerve tissue, once damaged, cannot be regenerated. The facts and my independent research projects prove otherwise.

Having seen unmistakable proof that persons considered incurable and totally irremediable return rather solidly and effectively to a state of health, I have come to this important, unalterable conclusion. To wit: There is hardly anything that is really incurable. Of course there are many ailments that are unreachable, but unreachable by the methods employed, which are not by any means the only methods available to the sick, despite the posturings and self-praising glorifications of the healing profession that denominates itself "the scientific community."

Why all this preamble? Because many doctors, and even doctors of some illustrious reputation, declare at times to patients with ailments they cannot reach: "Go home and forget about it; it is only your nerves." *Only* your nerves. Imagine! Just as though nerves were mere appendages rather than the Master System of the human body. All other systems in the human frame are subordinate to the nervous system. The respiratory and circulatory systems, the digestive and urinary systems, the lymphatic and endocrine systems—all are energized by and take their functioning directions from the nervous system.

So what follows is of utter importance: foods that can restore and feed and healthify nerves; foods that can nourish and rejuvenate the system that enables every other system in the body to perform.

It was just about the time when I concluded a research project indicating the importance of pecan nuts and lecithin and yeast and wheat germ as nerve foods, that into the office trooped that sad little elderly man with trifacial neuralgia. Mr. Karl's pain was almost unbearable, his ability to bear it almost impossibly heroic. If he had come to me a year earlier, before I had run independent tests on foods to regenerate nerve tissue, I doubt my ability to help him. As it was, merely by tractioning his head away from the shoulders to relieve direct nerve pressure and then giving him a program of foods specifically for that aching, hollering trigeminus nerve, in a short ten days he was free of pain and in five weeks entirely well, the condition not having returned when I checked him at six-month periods for several years. Yet all that the other doctors he had seen offered was either alcohol injections into the fifth cranial nerve, or cutting and severing it altogether.

The best single health-giving food for the nerves that I have ever found is pecans. Just raw and unsalted pecan nuts, about twelve to fifteen daily for desirable results. Pecans are rich in pyridoxine, which is a B-vitamin factor I have mentioned in other chapters. While wheat germ and soybeans are also very good sources of pyridoxine, and brewer's yeast is a close contender, it developed in my projects that pecans gave the best and quickest results—also the most lasting results—for reasons I cannot fathom. My theory would be that pecans worked best because they were easiest to handle as a food added to the diet, but this may be wrong. In any event, using Mr. Karl's example, the darting and throbbing pain along the skin of his face and even in his upper right teeth did not altogether cease with the other nerve foods, but on adding pecans it not only quieted but quit altogether.

It is hard to believe that even such heretofore unreachable nerve maladies as shaking palsy have been relieved merely by adding rather liberal quantities of pyridoxine-rich foods to the daily intake.

A portly, middle aged man named Brewster who was, as he called himself, "An incurable baseball nut," had a terrifying case of sciatica that pained both his left leg and his emotions because it prevented his attending the ball games. He had submitted to the local hospital's every physiotherapy modality, had had the nerve injected, had been tractioned and given heel lifts and everything else from short wave diathermy to ultrasound, but at most he enjoyed a half-day's respite from pain from any of it.

When I saw Brewster, his upper lip and brow were covered with big drops of perspiration, all from the pain from the left sacral area in his hip down through the calf to his ankle bone. I did a bit of tractioning also, although somewhat differently. When he lay flat on his back on the floor with the left leg, knee locked and stiff, up against the wall, this stretched the leg and shifted the aching sciatic nerve into the center of the sciatic notch and gave him some relief, not enough by any means. But when I asked him to inch closer to the wall, thus applying stronger traction to the leg which was boosted up against the wall, and also added a variety of nerve-feeding foods to his diet—well! Within a week his pains wound down and in two weeks he was bellowing his lungs out painlessly at the baseball games.

Two years later Brewster brought in his newlywed daughter who had developed epilepsy of the epileptoid (petit mal) variety, and upon questioning him he said, "What sciatica? I've never even had a shadow or hint of its return." When I asked if he still ate his daily portion of pecans and the other good nerve-nourishing foods he became utterly serious. "With all the pain I bore on and off for years, when I'm cured you can bet I know what cured me and I stay with the winning numbers. Those pecans, and that soybean that has lecithin in it, I almost never miss such miracle foods, and I rest against the wall for extra insurance, too."

For years I have asked people with nerve-induced sleeplessness to eat a handful of raw pecans during the day, others to consume about a dozen pecans at bedtime. Both worked equally well, it appeared. Eating raw, unsalted pecan nuts was a good dependable way to better, more restful sleep. The magic seemed to be in the 50 milligrams of natural, organic pyridoxine that the patients got into their systems by the pecan route. As few as ten pecans supply this amount.

For flavoring, I suggest a tablespoonful of blackstrap molasses, for this also supplies the desired amount of pyridoxine. Both pecans and blackstrap molasses feed the nerves; then sleep induced by them further rests the nerves. Moreover, in the case of blackstrap molasses, besides the pyridoxine content there is a rich added value of organic calcium, and calcium is known to promote good sleep. In difficult insomnia cases I sometimes advise a cup of warm water or skim milk to which is added a tablespoonful of blackstrap molasses.

FOODS THAT OVERCOME FRIGHT

It is well known that the B-vitamin foods are the dependable *stress foods*. Chief among them are brewer's yeast and wheat germ. If you are facing a task that causes you to become tense and a little frightened—something as unnerving, let us say, as making a public speech or giving an important dinner party— here is what to do. Take a teaspoonful of brewer's yeast stirred into a cup of fruit juice or skim milk and sip it slowly. That's one way. Another way to use a miracle food instead of an unnatural medicine is to eat a dozen raw pecan nuts. A third way is to eat a small dish of wheat germ cereal softened with plain yogurt, which liquefies it and makes it palatable. To add to the benefits of all this, sweeten it with a large spoonful of blackstrap molasses. Note this, and note it well. What you will have done by doing this is something extraordinarily wonderful in that you will have supplied your body, which is hungry for healing, natural substances with exactly what it needs to give strength to the nervous system.

Read and reread the paragraph above. Tell your friends about these natural ways to health, especially those friends given to nervous spasms and crying jags and even tantrums. *Be a funnel and not a reservoir.* Let good healthifying information flow through you, not be buried inside you. Just get your friends to try what is written above and then note what strength they have quite sanely and naturally given the nerve tissue of their entire body.

A MAGIC MIRACLE SPREAD

As in the case of Brewster with his horrendous sciatica and great enthusiasm for baseball, I devised a little magic miracle spread that I also used successfully with the elderly Mrs. Lucille. She had brought her husband to me for treatment, but she herself had a facial tic that needed attention. While we talked I could not keep my gaze away from her left eye, or the tissue just below the eye, that bounced and carried on as though it would hurl itself at you.

At first I recommended parsnips to her as a longevity nerve food, instructing her to steam the parsnips in a very little water and make a noonday meal of the vegetable along with a cupful of barley water. This helped to a degree, but not sufficiently. Alfalfa tea was added to her fare and it helped further, then rice water because of its pangamic content—all these drinks just warm and never drunk hot, or taken cool if desired and without fail sipped slowly, not gulped down the throat. Later blackstrap molasses was added as a sweetener, especially to the alfalfa tea, and when this was taken several times a day along with my tractioning the neck vertebrae by lifting the head off the shoulders for a minute or two, the eye really began to quit bouncing and carrying on.

The miracle did not come to pass, however, until we came to the magic miracle spread. I have already indicated the great value of lecithin, because it is, among other things, a constituent of every cell in the body, most especially nerve cells. The rich, very valuable source of lecithin is soybeans. By soaking soybeans overnight and then cooking them slowly over low heat, they can be mashed or blenderized into a spread and used on bread in the same way as butter. But then came the miracle touch. Pecans have the enormous additional value of pyridoxine. Sunflower seeds are the best source of vitamin A and almost the best protein to be found, and it is even a sex food because it powers the formation of male sperm. By grinding sunflower seeds *plus* pecan nuts and adding both to the mashed soybeans we have a nutty, flavorful spread.

Now suppose this miracle mixture is spread on wheat germ bread or toast. Within wheat germ is also a content of wheat germ oil, the value of which has been explained on previous pages. And suppose the person who consumes this also has a prostate gland problem, as is common with many men over forty. Then, adding to the miracle, one can also grind up in a little inexpensive nut grinder available at health food stores, an ounce or two of pumpkin seeds. Now you have a variety of unbelievably valuable health-givers: soybean lecithin, pecans, sunflower seeds, pumpkin seeds. Mixing this together with the soybean mash that acts as a base, you have a nutty spread over wheat germ bread that is a miracle medicine for the nerves impossible to beat or even equal.

EVERYONE NEEDS NERVE NUTRITION

From all of the foregoing there flowed into my head another thought. Suppose as an experiment I advised all patients, no matter what happened to be their complaints or problems, to consume each morning as a breakfast meal a few slices of wheat germ toast thickly spread with the flavorsome nutty spread outlined above, and have this along with a cup of water or skim milk flavored with a tablespoonful of blackstrap molasses. In this way I would add to the already superlative benefits the values of iron and the rest that is contained in the molasses. No matter what ailed a person, by consuming this rich combination, the body just had to respond in some degree and health ought to flow into the body as a consequence.

This is exactly what happened. It happened for a very solid and physiologically unassailable reason. In the human body the master system is the nervous system, which may be called the boss of the works. If anything at all went wrong with the body it was the nerves or the nervous system that went wrong to some extent at the same time. Therefore, went my reasoning, if I fed the nervous system with miracle longevity foods specifically proven to be nerve-nourishers, that would necessarily have to help all else that was wrong in the body. And here, in one fell swoop as they say, I had the world's best nerve-healing foods in one small breakfast package: pecans, soybean lecithin, black-strap molasses, sunflower and pumpkin seeds, even some wheat germ oil from the wheat germ bread. If I but added a daily teaspoonful of brewer's yeast I would have, as is said graphically, "the whole ball of wax."

THE CHOICEST, HEALTHIEST DRINKS

Mrs. Lucille, with her disturbing tic douloureux, obeyed most of the good instructions but held on to one bad habit—coffee. When I tractioned her neck to take the nerve pressure off her neck bones and recommended the miracle spread, she liked it so well that she ate the wheat germ toast with the nutty soybean spread several times a day, and the way her tic stopped was a marvel to behold. But she could not take the water into which was stirred a tablespoonful of molasses. "It's not that the taste is bad," she said, "but it's just that I can't seem to navigate without my coffee. However," she rationalized, "I've taken to drinking decaffeinated coffee, not the real stuff."

As indicated, the terribly annoying bounce in her left eye and surrounding tissue had ceased, and she was immensely pleased. But Mrs. Lucille's facial neuralgia had by no means completely given up. The left side of her gums still hurt a little, the left upper lip was still a bit numb, there remained a bother-some over-secreting duct in her left eye.

"Sorry to upset your cart," I told her, "but your prized decaffeinated coffee is, in my view, just as bad as real, pure (impure) coffee. It is coffee that has been monkeyed with. The additives needed to make it decaffeinated militate against using it, in my judgment. I would just as soon have my addicted patients drink the real, unadulterated stuff as the decaffeinated kind."

"So what is one to drink?" the disappointed lady wanted to know. "What, for instance, do you yourself drink?"

"Good question," I conceded. "I have four to five drinks that I can recommend. All of them are useful and none is harmful to the organism."

Mrs. Lucille listened hard. She admitted that she still missed the absence of full sensation in her tongue, and sometimes the pain when masticating, but felt so much improved already that there was hope for full recovery in her mind. If coffee was the remaining culprit she would, she guessed, gird her loins and give it up.

"There are several drinks I favor," and I ticked them off. "Warm water with a tablespoonful of blackstrap molasses would usually come first, unless there is a built-in distaste for the burnt-nut flavor. The bioflavonoid drink, warm or cool, is in my opinion next in value for most people. To make this drink most easily, I suggest you do this. Mix some frozen orange juice in the regular way by adding three glasses of water to the one can of frozen juice. Then pour a bit of this liquid into a blender together with one lemon that has been cut into small pieces, skin and pulp and all. Whirl the lemon around with the small amount of juice and then add it all to the entire four-glass mixture. Now you have a bioflavonoid drink that you can warm up to desired temperature or drink cool as a beverage.

"Alfalfa tea comes somewhere close in value, I think. In some cases I have observed extraordinary results just from having patients with nerve problems (and with various other ills) take as many as a dozen alfalfa tablets a day. This is strictly a food, so no one need think of taking twelve tablets as taking medicine. As tea, merely boil water and add a teaspoonful of alfalfa, or a bag or two of the prepared alfalfa leaves, and then flavor it all if you desire with lemon juice or honey.

"As a regular table drink, and as a between-meals drink, I have two quite valuable suggestions. Rice water and barley water. At the royal table in Britain, a flask of barley water is always served and ready says the author, who served the queen for many years. To make these drinks, one merely boils up the brown rice or whole barley, then drains off the water and lets it cool, refrigerating it in a jar until needed.

"Of course, I cannot in clear conscience recommend coffee in any form because of its caffeine content, and this goes for tea also because it contains both caffeine and tannic acid, and all this goes doubly for cocoa or chocolate."

When Mrs. Lucille stopped her coffee habit altogether the remaining pains quit altogether also. "I used to have a funny sensation when I took anything with salt," she said. "It was a kind of altered taste—very disagreeable. Now I have no tender or sensitive areas in any of the skin near my eye, and no spasms of pain at all. I could really say the miracle foods cured me."

MEMORY IS FICKLE

Some of this happened in my practice many years ago. I really enjoy a degree of total recall when it comes to cases, although I very often cannot for the life of me recall the names of the patients. It is as though their names were unimportant while what was the matter with them was indeed utterly important. In this case of tic douloureux I remember sitting the lady down for some final words of advice before letting her go.

"Memory is fickle, but paper never forgets so write down some of these things," I said to her. And then I went over the salient truths that she needed to hug to her breast, repeating things she already knew, because we have a habit of drifting back into old ways. I said to her, "If you repeat the sorry habits that caused your trouble in the first place, they will very likely bring on the same or similar troubles again."

I made it clear that nerve-disturbed patients are nearly always helped by adding vitamin E to the daily diet. I urged the consumption of from 400 to 800 International Units (I.U.s) every day, taking them after meals or at bedtime. Because wheat germ is a fine source of vitamin E, along with a host of other beneficial values for nerve-damaged patients, I generally advise taking wheat germ as the preferred cereal food at breakfast. In addition to the bowl of wheat germ, it is well to take about two tablespoonsful of lecithin flakes, available at health food stores and nowadays sometimes also at supermarkets. The lecithin flakes mix well with the wheat germ cereal. Both are truly excellent healing foods for the nerves.

It cannot be repeated too often that wheat germ *oil*—one teaspoonful daily—helps nearly every neurasthenic, neuritic and neuralgic patient. In severe cases it is well to take two spoonsful daily, one after breakfast and one at bedtime, thus assuring its healing presence in the bloodstream throughout the 24-hour period.

In afflictions of neuritis I have found the drinking of plain rice water to afford blessed relief even after other substances had failed. This means taking about four ounces of cooled-down rice water, sipped slowly, every hour of the waking day between mealtimes. It appears that the body can utilize fluids in four-ounce portions, but similar benefits do not show themselves when large tumblersful are drunk, especially when swallowed in big draughts instead of sipped.

It should be emphasized and reemphasized that when there is mental illness, an important food for the nerves and the brain's nerve cells is lecithin. Remember that a large piece of brain tissue is actually lecithin. When mentally disturbed persons are given liquid lecithin twice a day, at 12-hour intervals, they often improve so rapidly as to make psychologists, psychiatrists and psychoanalysts marvel and disbelieve. The miracle is that the healing value of the lecithin taken at 12-hour intervals is there nourishing the brain cells around the clock, always there to help the functions of the brain all day long. Lecithin is part of every nerve and nervule in the body, a constituent of the enveloping nerve sheath that so often is damaged in mental illness, and I simply cannot overurge the consumption of liquid lecithin (or lecithin flakes where the liquid is not tolerated) in every condition where nerve tissue is involved.

SUMMARY

Principal nerve food: RAW PECANS

Assisting miracle foods: LECITHIN (liquid or flakes)
                         SOYBEANS
                         WHEAT GERM (cereal)
                         WHEAT GERM OIL
                         BLACKSTRAP MOLASSES
                         BREWER'S YEAST
                         YOGURT
                         ALFALFA TEA
                         PARSNIPS
                         BARLEY WATER
                         RICE WATER
                         VITAMIN E (400–800 I.U.s)

14

Seven Foods That Often Renew and Revive Visual Health

There are in this country about 97 million people who have resigned themselves to wearing those crutches draped over the bridge of the nose that we call eyeglasses.

I have dealt with my share of them professionally. None that I can remember was ever told by his or her optometrist, occulist or ophthalmologist that visual acuity can be improved without glasses; that better eyesight can be achieved in many if not most cases to the point of not needing glasses at all. But independent researches have forced me to the view that dependence on eyeglasses may often be abandoned even in older people and in difficult problem cases. I am not guessing here, for I know this to be true. Working alone, without tax benefits or government aid or subsidies, I've often managed to achieve visual effectiveness and general ocular balance in hundreds suffering from various eye conditions who were dependent on eyeglasses but thereafter needed no glasses or professional help of any kind.

There are simple techniques that actually change the *shape* of the eyeball in human beings. They are little techniques, easy to do. They make seeing possible without the aid of glasses in cases where glasses had been thought necessary for the rest of one's days. How so? Changing the eyeball structurally is how it is done. When the beams of light entering the eye do not hit the correct retinal spot, the optician or refractionist grinds lenses to make possible the focusing of light rays on the retina. But when a few muscle-stretching drills pull the eyeball back into shape from its out-of-round state, the incoming light beams hit the retina properly and no glasses need be worn.

And when the eyeball change is achieved from the out-of-round shape to normal shape, then, as will be explained presently, there's magic in seven amazing healing foods for the eyes, chief among them being sunflower seeds. The others are carrots, kelp, fish liver oil, apricots, salmon and sweet potatoes.

I well remember Hortense, a lady of dowager mien who delighted in reciting to me how many illustrious specialists she had seen and how much money she had spent. "I am very impressed," I told her, "but I don't want to hear any more about them. You make them sound so illustrious and distinguished that if I hear any more I will want to imitate their procedures—and then I'd fail as they did." The lady's eyebrows arched in surprise. "Yes, my dear. The fact is that you still have 20/200 vision and still need those thick lenses that you say make you look ugly, so those eminent doctors you laud so loudly haven't helped you." I paused for emphasis. "You are here, aren't you?—no longer with them."

She got off her imperious horse then, and I sat her down for a small lecture.

"Here are the facts, madam. You do all your work using the front muscles of your eyes and the muscles of side vision hardly at all. You watch television right in front of you, you read and sew and write letters and do everything else with eyes fixed straight forward, so with the muscles of front vision pulling forward all the time and the muscles of side vision not counteracting by pulling on the eyeballs sideways, what do you think happens? It tends to elongate the eyeballs. From front to back it pulls the spherical structures forward. So you can imagine the result. The light rays do not hit the seeing spot in back of the eye, for by overworking the front muscles you've pulled the eyeballs out-of-round and created a distance between where the rays converge and where the retina actually is. Do you understand this simple explanation?"

Hortense nodded. It was the first time anyone had ever taken the time to make optics or vision clear to her.

"Now we're going to force you to use the peripheral muscles of your eyes—those lazy side muscles which have fallen into disuse. While your husband drives you here and everywhere else, and you are not the driver but the passenger, reach into the glove compartment for a folded map or a three-by-five index card, then place it against your nose and eyebrows to shut out central vision. With the card against your nose you cannot see ahead but can see out of each side, and you can count the passing telephone poles or cars or trees or houses on both sides as you whiz by. By thus looking only sideways, the muscles of your side vision will be working. Being weak from underwork, in a few minutes those peripheral muscles will get tired as you keep seeing out of the sides. When this occurs you can rest the structures in the following way. Squeeze the eyelids tightly together, which squeezes the tired blood out of the capillaries, then open with a blinking or fluttering motion, which causes the capillaries to widen and new fresh blood nutrition for the eyes rushes in. By doing this several times you set up a pumping action onto the eyes—squeeze out the old and rush in the new blood. It revives tired eyes in a hurry."

"Sounds logical," said Hortense in a whisper, seemingly impressed. "What then? And how often do I do this? And for how long?"

"Not so fast," I countered. "There are other items you have to grasp first. Ahead of everything else you must *get the idea, then all else will follow.* Soak up fully and completely the value of exercising the muscles of side vision so hard and so often that they will pull your elongated eyeballs back into rounded shape, so the light rays can hit the retina correctly and good vision becomes possible without having lenses ground to a couple or three or six diopters of correction to make seeing happen. Meanwhile, on this program of ours, your eye structures will be nourished *specifically* by some amazing healing foods. Vitamin-rich sunflower seeds for one, because of their appropriable vitamin A content. Also red salmon and kelp for the balanced minerals you need, and at least a daily tablespoonful of cod liver oil taken when it does not mix with any other food or drink, and if all goes well you should enjoy a measure of eyesight you thought impossible at your age."

That was exactly how it went. Our elegant Lady Hortense altered her demeanor and became an advocate of what she labeled "Nature's Path to Sight Sans Spectacles," a subject she used as lecture material at her Women's Club, going at it like an enlightened missionary with a glowing torch.

At first her eyes bothered her even more than previously. She went to her occulist and was informed that it was because, "for some mysterious reason," she needed weaker rather than stronger lenses and those she wore had *unaccountably* become too strong for her. This was a mere few weeks after she had started on the program. Later, her eyes required another change to even weaker lenses, and finally she needed no help at all. She could see and read and do her work without glasses at all! All this in a woman of near 60 who had worn glasses since adolescence—and all of it changed in six months.

Hortense did the self-aligning exercises, all of which unpinched the nerve pressures she had accumulated over the years of straining and turning and twisting and getting jarred and jolted. This enabled her metabolic functions to operate in high altitude and her system could fully assimilate the amazing healing properties in the foods she was advised to eat. The healing foods which she consumed over the six-month period so beneficially nourished her weak eyes that she regained the visual purple of a normal person. She could spot an empty seat in a dark movie house as quickly as anybody. Although the lady continued to carry a pair of reading glasses "strictly from long-conditioned fear," she said, they were insurance she did not use and still could hardly believe her ability to read all but the smallest and finest print entirely without glasses.

Curiously enough, the eyewash remedies which Hortense had tried earlier and for a time gave her relief were abandoned in a few months because the aid was temporary. The herbal eyewashes did indeed cleanse the debris out of her eye structures, but they could not and did not change the distorted *shape* of the eyeballs. Eyewashes, however temporarily helpful, cannot alter the shape of the eyeballs, and normal vision can follow only when eyeball shapes are changed from out-of-round to correct front-to-back distance. Unlike the short-lived relief Hortense experienced with the highly touted eyewashes, our program gave lasting aid; for when I saw her again two or three years later, the lady was free of eye problems and continued with unabated enthusiasm to give lectures to Women's Clubs on "Sight Sans Spectacles."

TECHNIQUES FOR CHANGING EYE STRUCTURES

In ways similar to Hortense, Adelle was a lady in her mid-50s with progressive myopia and frequent conjunctivitis of the follicular variety, also wealthy and proud of having consulted only the "big men" in the eye-healing profession, all to no avail. Like Hortense she'd been sentenced to wearing thick lenses that made her appear unattractive she thought, but what was there to do? All her doctors followed conventional patterns and none either subscribed to or ever mentioned changing the *shape* of the eyeball to change its visual capability. Also like Hortense, Adelle kept repeating how eminent her specialists were until I insisted that if they had also been successful she would not have had to come to me seeking eye health. This was a lady sadly in need of a new focus on the matter of regaining and maintaining full visual capacity: the trick of strengthening peripheral vision for one, the uses of the Miracle Health Promoter M for another, and the incalculably great value of the amazing healing foods—all of these approaches never studied by medical eye specialists of the "regular" school and outside their province of expertise.

Accordingly, I outlined a few effective techniques for changing the out-of-round shape of the eyeballs (as given above in the case of Hortense) along with the specific foods for the eyes, a matter which Adelle said was worth thousands of dollars because she had never before heard of such magic as food for the eyes. With great enthusiasm she followed all directions. *In two months Adelle's thick eyeglasses needed to be scaled down to ordinary thin ones.* In another two months even these became a bother and she discovered she could read happily and comfortably with no glasses at all except for what they called small 5-point print. The program that achieved this was as follows.

A card was placed in front of her eyes to shut out central vision and force her to see out of the sides and thus make her peripheral eye muscles strong. This was perhaps the most creative exercise in remolding the shape of the lady's eyes. Also, as in the case of Hortense and all such out-of-round conditions in eyeball shapes, Adelle was instructed to rest the eyes that had become quickly weary from this unaccustomed peripheral exercise by tightly squeezing the eyelids shut and then opening them with a rapid flutter or blinking motion. With her background of bouts with conjunctivitis she needed to pump fresh healing blood into the eye regions by this squeeze-and-flutter eyelid exercise more often than most.

After quite tiring the muscles of Adelle's side vision by the card in front of the eyes technique and by "thinking sideways," I advised her to rest them from their performing unaccustomed work after years of non-use by applying cool cloths over closed eyelids. This was best done by wetting a handkerchief-sized washcloth under the tap (no colder than tap water), then lying down for a 5-to-10-minute rest period with the cloths over the closed eyes. This relaxed the eyes and constricted the capillaries soothingly for a short time.

Additionally, she was to shut out light from time to time by crossing her palms over the bridge of the nose and completely covering her eyes for another 5-minute stretch. It is now understood by sophisticated physiologists in up-to-the-minute studies that when the eyes relax and rest so also does the entire body tend to relax and rest.

The advice to "think sideways" brought a surprised comment from Adelle. "What's that?" she said in rising inflection. It was the same question asked by Hortense when I recommended this helpful technique.

It happened that both Hortense and Adelle were theater- and concert-goers. To further strengthen the muscles of their side vision I counseled them to close their eyes when seated in the theater and "see" the people on each side as they sat in adjoining seats. As they beheld the seated people on each side in their mind's eye, the peripheral muscles also automatically pulled to each side and worked to reshape the eyeballs from the out-of-round to normal spherical shape. Then followed the technique of opening their eyes to look at the theater curtain in front, but at the same time also widening their eyes consciously until they could also "see" the people in the adjacent seats. It is a trick easily learned after a few attempts. In one moment they found they could see three objects: the curtain in front and each person on the sides. This, they were told, is both thinking sideways and working their eye muscles sideways, thereby exercising heretofore underworked peripheral muscles.

Another way to forcefully strengthen their visual side muscles was this. Seated comfortably they looked at an object in front, say a picture or table ornament; then they separated their arms to each side and wiggled the fingers of each hand, seeing the wiggling fingers on the sides while at the same time also watching the object in front. As their arms went farther apart the side muscles of vision were stretched and more strongly exercised as their eyes saw the moving fingers on each side while also watching the central object. This exercise in short order accomplishes a change in the shape of human eyeballs that nothing in conventional treatment can achieve. If this is done at night, just before retiring, the gains are maintained during sleep when the organism attends to repairing bodily damage.

Still another emphatic recommendation was the matter of rolling the eyes within closed lids both clockwise and counterclockwise, stretching them as far as possible in every direction while the eyes are being bathed in their own lubricating fluid. The thing to do is imagine a huge clock. The hour of twelve is way up high, three is far off to the right side, six requires the eyes to stretch very far down below one's feet, then far to the left to see the hour of nine. Doing this in both directions, clockwise and counterclockwise until tired, gives those weak peripheral muscles a needed workout and strongly pulls the out-of-round eye structures back into normal shape.

"Three things you must unfailingly take note of," I counseled. "One, you must not stare. Two, you must use often and vigorously the muscles of side vision. Three, you must learn to use your eyes almost like balls rolling within their sockets, rolling them in both directions, and doing this often if you use your eyes a lot, thus bathing them frequently in their natural healing fluids within the sockets."

I ticked off the three items, using different emphases.

THREE PRINCIPAL RULES FOR BETTER VISION

"Don't stare. To halt this habit, learn to see without looking. Note these three words: *See without looking.* Instead of trying to stare at an object, let it flow into the camera radius of your eyes. A camera makes no effort to see, and neither should you. A camera merely lets an object or scene flow into the range of its open lens. If you look at your outstretched finger, do not stare at the knuckle or nail or wrinkled skin, but just allow all of the finger to roll into your range of vision. See the finger without really looking at it. To stare is to hurt the eyes. Do not stare.

"Second, you must make the muscles of your peripheral vision so strong that they equal the pull of the front muscles which you use in reading, typing, TV viewing, sewing and such. This ensures your maintaining the eyeball in-the-round, and then the light beams that enter the eye can converge where they should inside the eye structure and you will not need spectacles to make them converge there. To achieve this you ought to try to think sideways every day. Every now and then you ought to shut off central vision with the card that forces you to use the side muscles by seeing sideways, and you ought to wiggle your fingers as you spread your hands and see the wiggling fingers sideways. The farther you spread those wiggling fingers, the more you will stretch and strengthen the muscles of side vision.

"Third, you must roll your eyes as often as you can and bathe them in their own natural healing and cleansing fluid; also stretch them within closed lids as far up and down and to the sides as you can, doing this both clockwise and counterclockwise, especially at bedtime. And after a tiring drill of this kind you ought to rest the eyes by first tightly squeezing the lids and then opening them with a swift fluttering motion.

"Last, as you nourish those poor wanting eye structures of yours (that you overwork every day in artificial light and un-natural straight-in-front pull and strain) with the amazing and well-tested healing foods such as sunflower seeds, a daily teaspoonful of kelp, a meal now and then of about three ounces of red salmon scooped out of cans, and carrots of either the raw or steamed kind for their carotene to help the visual purple of the eyes, fish liver oil for their superlative vitamin A content, and sweet potatoes as perhaps the most desirable cooked vegetable for eye sufferers, plus apricots as perhaps the best fruit—as you take on all this magical nourishment plus a daily salad of greens topped with a bit of plain yogurt and a teaspoonful of wheat germ oil, be sure to employ the Miracle Health Promoter M. These exercises will thereby work toward self-aligning a structurally misaligned body, unpinch nerve pressures in the spine and assure your system's ability to absorb, utilize and assimilate *in the cells* the wonders in the amazing foods you are ingesting."

The list of desirable foods was not limited to the abovementioned items. It included such assisting healing foods as cold pressed soya or safflower oil in addition to the teaspoonful of wheat germ oil in the plate of salad greens. Also have daily rations of plain nonfruit yogurt, watercress, collards, mustard greens, turnip and dandelion greens, occasionally raw pecan nuts as an entire protein meal of seeds, either whole or gound if chewing is a problem, using two or three ounces of sunflower seeds, sesame seeds or pumpkin seeds in place of such protein items as wheat germ, soy beans, fish, etc.

After the fourth month Adelle came in once a month for a checkup and continued to enjoy life without glasses. To hear this erstwhile tough-talking lady say it, "I'm full of beans in my new-found life." Then she would arch one eyebrow slyly and say, "I'm an S-lady, did you know it? Full of S-S-S's." My expression showed that I did not understand. "Easy," she explained jauntily. "I am Seriously, Studiously Serene and Sanguine Sans Spectacles." I noted the series of words that began with the letter S and realized she used this in her talks to Women's Clubs on Visual Health without Glasses.

MIRACLE FOODS REVERSE LEGAL BLINDNESS

Despite their initial resistance to natural healing methods neither Hortense nor Adelle gave me any trouble once they got the idea. I had told them if they once captured the idea of amazing healing foods and possessed the technique for reshaping the eyeball structure, then all else would follow. Not so with Randolph, a brother in my Masonic lodge who had lost so much sight that he'd been declared legally blind. He was a dispirited man, forever despondent and critical of everything and believing in almost nothing at all.

"Then why do you come to me?" I asked, reminding him of Oscar Wilde's remark that the critic knows the price of everything but the value of nothing. "Why are you here if you do not believe that anything can help you and if you think that for the rest of your days someone must lead you around? In your place I wouldn't bother to seek further treatments at all."

My own seemingly heartless cynicism must have got to Randolph, since it matched his own. He rationalized that it was well and good for me to be philosophical, but if I'd lost the world of seeing I too would be cantankerous, as I said he was.

"But Randolph, there are many blind people who are happy people," I pointed out. "I'm not sure that with your self-defeating, negative attitude you deserve the effort, but since you're a lodge brother I will take the time to give it this one shot—I'll spell out the actual chances for you. Will you listen?"

He listened. He mumbled something about having heard that I talked to patients in an honest no-nonense manner, and he listened quite carefully. I think there was something in my eyes and voice that said this was his last chance for personal, professional, humane and very caring attention, so that's what he gave me in return—his full eager attention.

I began with what I thought should be the beginning of eye-knowledge for unschooled people, and here's in essence what I told him.

"Most of us, Randolph, do not realize the vast energy disbursements we make through our eyes every day. Our eyes are enormously vascular, they are loaded with blood vessels, they need a lot of blood nutrition if only because we overwork them very much in the artificial light of our civilized world. Besides this, we stare and read and write and sew and watch TV with eyes glued straight in front of us, which overstrains the front eye muscles. This pulls the spherical eyeballs out-of-round towards the front. At the same time we *underwork* the side muscles of our vision, for our civilization has not made it necessary for us to employ much of our peripheral vision. We don't very much look to the sides or around corners the way animals and children do. So our eyes get misshaped, distorted, unable to see without corrective lenses. Are you following me, Randolph? Are you beginning to understand the trouble?"

The elderly man, listening very quietly and rigidly, nodded assent. "Every word," he said. "Glad to hear all this."

"Good, Randolph. In your case it is all a matter of degree. In your case the misshapen, distorted situation of your eyes has gone so far that you can hardly see at all."

"I understand," he said.

"Any wonder then," I continued, "that your eyes need a special workout and special nourishment more than most! Any wonder that the badly misshaped eyeballs in your head need to be reshaped? Is it becoming clear to you that so long as the eye doctors stick to drugs and their really great surgical procedures they will never really get at the root cause of eye problems in our civilization—that they will never reshape human eyeballs to where seeing becomes possible without glasses? Not drugs, and not even the best surgery will do that. None of it can get us ahead of the huge national build-up of eye problems and our increasing millions who are eyeglass wearers."

IF DRUGS COULD CURE, ALL WOULD BE WELL

I sat myself down opposite Randolph and in the quiet of the office with all the staff gone I gave him a long-remembered lesson.

"If their drugs cured, everyone would be well, since the pharmacopeia has drugs for every kind and variety of ailment. Yet eye troubles rise rather than diminish. The body manufactures all its own cortisone and insulin and adrenalin and pepsin and hydrochloric acid and its enzymes and secretions and everything else it needs for its health and growth. So what we need to do is to return the body that has become misshapen or distorted or out of whack to the shape where it can again manufacture its own natural chemicals (or drugs), and not rely on outside drugs that enrich pharmaceutical interests. As one writer put it: 'If drugs cure, why does anyone die except of old age?'

"If you get this idea, Randolph, you will be a good patient with a fair chance of getting back some good sight, perhaps all of it. Surgery itself does not cure but often does an excellent job of repairing what drugs cannot help. The failure of the physician is the opportunity of the surgeon. First of all you consult a physician. If his prescriptions cured you, you would have no need to go on to a surgeon. The rise in surgery attests to the failure of the physician's drugs. Your road to health is not by way of drugging the eyes but getting them back to their former proper shape in a natural way. Do you understand what I am saying?"

"I do," he said, and for the first time there was high enthusiasm in his voice.

"Good. So now what we will aim for is to get those eyeballs of yours back into correct shape from their out-of-round shape, and give them those amazing, specific, healing foods that they will soak up as avidly as a dry sponge soaks up water. Such foods will be the building blocks that your eyes need for their returning health. And—of great importance—you will be required to do the drills that we call the Miracle Health Promoter M, for they will put your bodily framework into correct alignment and enable you to fully utilize the healing benefits of those amazing foods."

I ticked off what I required this legally blind man to do. One, perform the eye exercises that tended to bring the eyeballs back into their normal spherical shape. Two, eat the amazing healing foods that were the building blocks for the eye structures. Three, do the drills of the Miracle Health Promoter M that would replace his entire body in the kind of alignment that was free of pinched nerves and made regaining health possible.

The man was ready for all of it; my taking time to lay out the facts brought him round to enthusiastic cooperation. First I introduced him to sunflower seeds as an eye-nourisher to cheer about, then to carrots for their valuable vitamin A content, also to greens such as mustard greens and turnip tops because they contain the needed carotene the same as carrots, and to yellow vegetables and fruits such as sweet potatoes and apricots. "It is the carotene in these foods that converts into vitamin A in your system, and it's needed for strong healthy eyes," I reminded him.

I stressed the value of vitamin A in its natural form, as it occurs in sunflower seeds and carrots and fish liver oil, for I had seen the mere addition of sunflower seeds to the diet clear up skin blemishes even in severe, pus-oozing acne. It needed to be emphasized that for all their healing power there were never any side effects from the amazing seeds and fruits and vegetables I introduced to Randolph's diet. Anyone who ever agonized over an itching anus, or the brutally debilitating effects of vaginal pruritus, as these conditions are called, knows the unforgettable value of sunflower seeds when responding more quickly and lastingly to a daily four ounces of these seeds than to drugs, with their temporary relief and often permanent side effects.

In areas close to the eyes, as in the roaring or hissing noises in the ears which are named tinnitus, sunflower seeds are often authentic magic when taken along with a few self-aligning exercises.

I warned against taking mineral oil as a laxative, for it destroys the precious vitamin A in the body, an example of what I meant by the untoward side effects of drug items.

"If you have ever been prescribed any antibiotic drugs," I said to him, "you need to know about sunflower seeds in combination with yogurt as a two-pronged road to gaining and maintaining health. Not only do the antibiotic drugs kill the protective lactic acid bacilli that we need in the system for intestinal health (because they hold down the fungi and prevent fungus infections), but by killing off these protective microorganisms you allow the fungi to grow and set up such states as itching rectal areas, irritated tongue tissues, athlete's foot and broken corners of the mouth and such. Since these conditions are almost always fungus-associated, I urge people to take yogurt to renew the helpful intestinal flora, and also sunflower seeds for their potent vitamin A content—both to be taken after any course of antibiotic treatments."

Randolph, I felt, also needed to know very clearly the part that raw pecan nuts must play in his eating program. To take about a dozen a day, I pointed out, is to consume a specific healing food for the nerves (see Chapter 13, Foods That Can Often Regenerate Damaged Nerves), and since the health of one's optic nerves foretells the health of one's vision it follows that a good, well-researched and tested food for the nerves such as pecans serves as a dependable healing item, particularly since it contains a rich supply of vitamin A while other nuts are surprisingly poor in this vitamin.

A small warning was necessary at this point. "As you re-shape your eyeball structures under my directions," I told him, "your eyes may smart or burn or itch while they return to normality. If this happens, Randolph, I'll order you to give up eating all protein-rich foods for about a week or two except for a daily meal of four ounces of sunflower seeds, which you may fine-grind to powder if you have trouble chewing the seeds from which the hulls, of course, have first been removed. By taking this amount of hulled sunflower seeds as your sole daily protein meal, and adding it to a large plate of raw salad greens topped with a dollop of plain yogurt, one teaspoon of wheat germ oil and a tablespoonful of cold-pressed soya or safflower oil, and also adding a bit of powdered kelp in place of the usual table salt, you will feel within one week a lessening of the smarting or burning. And if all goes well, this protein-limited week or two will hasten the reshaping drills in returning the eyeballs back into the round."

Randolph concentrated on all I said and appeared to re-member every instruction. It happened that he preferred sun-flower seeds to other proteins such as fish or soy beans or wheat germ, so it was no effort to stay on the program for the desired two weeks. After this short period of reshaping his eyeballs and living on the foods outlined above I suggested that he change to a more varied and less monotonous fare, but he declined. He was beginning to distinguish figures. In so incredibly small a time space his outlook changed from despondency to genuine hope. When I counseled a more rounded change of diet he urged me to let him stay on this program forever, for the results thus far were promising.

After one month on the program the elderly, cane-tapping man reported being able to see faces, then the features of the faces in detail, and after the tenth week he said he could "even count the wrinkles" in my forehead. Soon after the tenth week my front office nurse popped her head into my consulting room with, "His Highness, Sir Randolph, is on the phone and de-mands to speak to you personally." Like the others on the staff she did not like Randolph because of the bad time he gave them all in his cantankerous days.

"Yes, Randolph, what is it?" I asked.

"I'm downstairs here in the phone booth in the building of my ophthalmologist," he yelled. "He says I'm no longer legally blind. *I can see normally*! He says I might have been faking my blindness until now."

HELP FOR CATARACTS AND GLAUCOMAS

The program set forth above was not peculiar to blindness or to myopia or astigmatism or anything like that. Others with glaucoma and cataract problems responded to almost the same program, for the most part.

In glaucoma they suffer from an intraocular pressure that not only is often unbearable but can hurt the optic nerve by reason of this transferred pressure. For this I devised a simple routine that proved immensely helpful. The patients were asked to rub their hands together quite briskly, thus creating a pile-up of static electricity. When the hands were sufficiently heated in this manner they quickly applied the palms, or heels of the hands, to the closed lids, giving the hardened eyeball structures the value of one's own body heat. Moreover, this closed the body's own electrical circuit and offered the advantage of the laying on of hands. The latter is entirely natural and really useful—note how one naturally and automatically reaches up with the hands to contact the closed lids when the eyes hurt or burn or itch.

Heated hands, thus applied by glaucoma patients to the closed lids, gave them the feeling, if done several times a day, that the pressure within the eye was giving way, that it was lightening and letting up, that the eyeball was becoming softer and providing a degree of relief, and all quite naturally, without drugs. Often their occulists, using the instrument to measure intraocular pressure, told glaucoma patients that "something was happening" to reduce the inner pressure.

In many cases the night vision of these cases improved in merely one month on the program of consuming the healing foods and reshaping the eyeballs. They complained of fewer blind spots or rainbow patterns. It was a revelation to them that this could happen, and that such incredible cures could take place, so quickly and without any surgery or drugs.

In cataract cases, as in glaucoma, salt was forbidden because it tended to close the capillaries that conveyed blood nutrition to the eyes. But liberal sprinklings of powdered kelp could take the place of salt. Also large portions of brewer's yeast were taken to supply a potent vitamin B content.

Cataract sufferers discover that their ability to see is lessened because there is a thickening or clouding of the lens of the eye. As a useful drink I've found unsalted tomato juice taken in four ounce doses and sipped slowly every waking hour of the day to be the best for reasons I cannot explain. After about two weeks of this, the change to carrot juice offered even more help. In addition to sunflower seeds, I advise an occasional change to sesame seeds, whole or ground; sometimes a mix of the two if preferred. Besides the seeds as the chief source of nutrition for eye cases, the other amazing healing foods, such as carrots, sweet potatoes, fish liver oil and the others listed at the end of this chapter, plus the Miracle Health Promoter M drills, often made such a change *in a single month of the program* that many cataract cases reported a declouding in the lens of their eyes and a genuine ability to see better.

I observed one odd thing about cataract patients, namely that there was a speedier return to unclouded vision when they did the peripheral muscle exercises vigorously every hour on the hour, and following the ensuing tiredness applied cold cloths over the eyelids for five-minute rest periods. Also, bioflavonoid drinks appeared to speed results. Some used as much as two lemons a day with skin and all mixed in some orange juice, and this reportedly made results come faster. Moreover, I learned that an occasional change from sunflower seeds to red salmon (canned) as the main protein item of nutrition was advisable after the initial two-week period, as though there was a need in many cases of some form of flesh protein.

Every patient with eye problems was given a list of allowable and especially helpful foods when he or she was discharged—the list summarized below. Some wandered into the office years later with folded and faded papers bearing the list, requesting a new copy because the first had been consulted so often and faithfully that it almost wore out and they feared being without this "amazing anchor," as they called it.

SUMMARY

Principal healing food for the eyes: SUNFLOWER SEEDS

Six other amazing eye foods: CARROTS

SALMON

FISH LIVER OIL

YOGURT

KELP

SWEET POTATOES/APRICOTS

Assisting healing foods: BREWER'S YEAST

WHEAT GERM OIL

WATERCRESS

TOMATO JUICE (unsalted)

TURNIP TOPS

MUSTARD GREENS

COLLARDS

RAW PECAN NUTS

BIOFLAVONOID DRINKS

CARROT JUICE

DANDELION GREENS

SESAME SEEDS

PUMPKIN SEEDS

VITAMIN C (2–4 grams a day)

SOY BEANS

SOYA OIL (cold pressed)

SAFFLOWER OIL (cold pressed)

Do not drink, or bathe eyes in tap water, but only distilled water.

15

Three Outstanding Throat-Healthifying Foods

For those who are subject to sore throats, and for those who suffer a lingering sore throat after every common cold, the specific marvel among miracle foods beyond question is the delicious pineapple.

Those, especially, who are troubled by a persistent hoarseness must read and heed what is written here. Hoarseness may be an advance sign of serious oncoming pathology, even cancer. It is always useful and often lifesaving to know what to do for a less than healthy throat and/or voice that is natural and effective, and that has no possibility of hurting us through side effects that may be worse than the original problem.

Pineapple must in all cases be of the very ripe variety. And I refer here to fresh pineapple, never canned. Other miracle foods for the throat are persimmons, kelp, honey that is taken raw and in small doses, rather than in large amounts, lest it slow down liver function in common with all sweets. But by far the most useful and miracle-working natural food for the throat is ripe pineapple.

Curiously, only the ripe pineapple contains bromelin, about which I wish to speak. I say curiously, because in the case of papaya, for example, the valuable papain that digests down uneliminated protein to its normal end products of digestion, exists in the slightly unripe papaya and is lost when the fruit turns very ripe and sugary.

In affections of the throat there is another vitally important matter to know about and heed very strictly. It is not a food, also not something to use but something to avoid. I refer to hot fluids and hot foods. I have found that they blister the delicate lining of the throat and must be shunted aside, never drunk or eaten.

I am thinking of the recent case of Rudy Vallee. For several decades Rudy Vallee has been a national celebrity, a gifted singer and band leader and entertainer who was star of the stage, motion pictures, television and radio, bringing joy to millions with his talents. But he found he had trouble with his voice, especially in the lower register. He did not know until he read a chapter on hot foods and fluids in a book of mine that the cause lay in consuming very hot soups every mid-day, which was his habit.

The book was *Doctor Morrison's Miracle Guide to Pain-Free Health and Longevity,* published by Parker Publishing Company. In it he read of my own experience, which triggered the research into hot foods and drinks. I had accidently dipped my forefinger into a cup of hot tea and withdrew it in a split second with a painful, "Ouch!" It started me thinking. My forefinger is protected by two layers of tough skin further subdivided into six layers and it has been case-hardened by exposure to hot and cold, rough and smooth, coarse and soft surfaces. Yet I could not stand the immersion of this well-protected finger for a second in fluid that I didn't deem too hot to throw down my gullet. In the second or two it took this very hot tea to get from my mouth to the stomach, it contacted and blistered by contact, the very delicate one-layer lining of the esophagus, to say nothing of the stomach itself and the delicate cobwebby lining of the mouth, lips, tongue and the rest.

Besides being a first-rank entertaining talent Rudy Vallee is a man of analytical intelligence. He saw at once that hot things contacting the mucous membrane of the throat caused a blistering effect. (Why hadn't other doctors reasoned this and come to this simple conclusion?) He understood also, that before the poor blistered mucous membrane lining could heal itself, down came another cup of hot coffee or tea or soup, blistering it all over again. He quit taking his beloved hot soups, put a stop to contacting his poor abused inner throat lining with other hot beverages or foods and, presto, the trouble ended. He was cured. He felt so strongly about this easy way to help others with singing careers (including his friend Frank Sinatra) and throat trouble that he wrote the publishers about it and asked them to send him my residence address. He has generously permitted the use of the letter, so I quote it here.

Dear Friends at Book Distributors:

I am writing about Dr. Marsh Morrison. For a long time I have observed his brilliant common sense analysis.

But it was only recently when I read the chapter on Hoarseness and Hot Foods that I realized his true near-genius in finding answers to difficult medical and physical questions.

For a long time I have been plagued with a vocal problem which has been entirely eliminated after reading that chapter in his book, Pain-Free Guide to Health and Longevity.

I recently mailed to Frank Sinatra (in Palm Springs) Xerox copies of that chapter, because it was very evident to me, as I listened to him on his 40th Anniversary TV Show, *that he was having difficulty in sustaining some of his notes, especially the low notes.*

His lawyer, Milton Rudin, mailed Frank a copy of my letter in which I stated that I was going to write Frank about a discovery that has helped me in my vocal problems!

I should receive a letter from Sinatra soon, as I know that he is appreciative of advice that might help him.

I am going to spread the gospel about Morrison not only on the radio and TV interviews . . . but when I talk to anyone who might appreciate a really important fact not understood by those of us who survive by our voices.

Truly, Dr. Morrison is a very intelligent and gifted man (and) I would appreciate receiving his residence address.

Sincerely,   *Rudy Vallee*

Later, when Rudy Vallee sent me permission to quote the foregoing letter, he wrote the following note:

> *It is a privilege and pleasure to add my comment and testimo-*
> *nial to your theory (about hot foods). My voice can now sustain no*
> *matter how much I have taxed it.*

The chief reason why ripe pineapple is, in my opinion, the foremost miracle food for throat ailments is that the bromelin it contains is a proteolytic enzyme, which means that it hastens the splitting or conversion of proteins into end products acceptable to the ailing cells. Bromelin is really a ferment something like the protein enzyme trypsin, that ultra-important enzyme charged with the job of reducing the protein foods you eat into simpler substances that can be utilized by the cells. In addition, it splits away from the utilizable portions of the foodstuff the other portions which are putrefactive and not needed or wanted by the system. If this sounds unwarrantably technical it only means that in fresh ripe pineapple there exists this ingredient, bromelin, that has tested out wonderfully in diseased and sore throats because it works on sick tissue while not affecting healthy tissue at all—a rare and miraculous occurrence.

Here is how it helps you.

Consider that you have a seriously sick sore throat. It is swollen on the inside, feels full of pus and other diseased matter, as though you had quinsy or a badly suppurating tonsillitis. How can you get ripe pineapple to work for you?

You slice small portions of the pineapple and apply them to the diseased tissue, holding them in contact as close as you can for as long as you can. If this is inconvenient you can squeeze fresh pineapple into juice and gargle for as long as possible with the juice contacting the sick areas. If you use the sliced pineapples you chew the little slices well but you do not swallow them. If you use the juice you gargle with it in contact with the sick tissue, but then you spit out the used-up juice and do not swallow it. What happens is that the bromelin in the pineapple contacts the unhealthy throat tissues and *works on the diseased cells,* digesting them down. It digests and reduces the diseased parts down to non-injurious substances, but it does not in any way affect healthy tissue adversely.

I recall the rather remarkable case of Timothy, a shoe salesman with a long-standing case of hoarseness. It embarrassed him. He felt that it interfered with his selling ability. But he did not attribute any serious disease such as cancer on the way because of it. I was treating him for a backlash injury to his neck, not at all for the hoarseness. But it concerned me and I thought it wise to let him feel my concern. This middle-aged man was a kind of devil-may-care fellow, not usually of serious mein, and in my judgment it helps with such people to let them know the seriousness of their problem or you get no proper cooperation. When I told Timothy about the real importance of his throat problem he abided the program and returned to health in a surprisingly short time.

Merely by gargling with ripe pineapple juice morning and night, Timothy's throat felt better and his hoarseness lightened a little. But it persisted while I treated his whiplash, which gave way easily. All I had to do was align the vertebrae of his neck and take the strain off the powerful SCM muscles that pulled his head offside, and this trouble was gone. An easy way to self-align every vertebra in his neck was a technique I taught him to do at home. Placing the palms of both hands on each side of his head at about the level of the ears he lifted the head off the shoulders, turning the head to left and then right as he did this. If someone was there to help with this, he or she could do the head-lift drill for him while he slowly turned the chin in both directions. If this was done several times daily, and especially at bedtime when he could rest the neck structures in a horizontal position afterward for a few hours, the vertebrae that were whiplashed out of adjustment tended to realign themselves and in a week or so he was well. His friend, who was in the same automobile bangup, said Timothy, went to a conventional drug-prescribing doctor who gave him diathermy treatments and pills, still suffered a month after the accident. But although the whiplash responded quickly, some of the hoarseness continued.

It was then that I told our hail-fellow salesman to quit all hot beverages and steaming, piping-hot foods. Continued hoarseness may well be a precursor of throat cancer, I informed him. I further advised him to bring in his wife so I could tell her the same thing, for wives, I have found, are really the "men behind the guns" in getting their menfolk well. When Timothy's wife was fully informed she took charge of her spouse's eating and within ten days his voice became a clear baritone—a remarkable case.

In some throat cases goitre is an unwelcome companion. If goitre is feared, or if it has already begun to form, I advise the use of powdered kelp. This helps in both the external goitres and those inner ones which cause the eyes to protrude, the condition labeled exophthalmia or exophthalmic goitre. The mineral content of kelp includes the finest kind of organic iodine for the thyroid gland.

"Give up all use of table salt," I told Timothy's wife, "but see that Tim shakes plenty of powdered kelp out of what used to serve as the salt shaker. If you think that iodized salt helps, forget the ads that say this. Instead, sprinkle the kelp on salads and into soups quite liberally. You can easily purchase powdered kelp at any health food store."

It was then that I followed my custom of giving small lectures to my patients, only in this case it was to Timothy and his wife.

"If persimmons are in season, I recommend them as the favorite dessert. Besides pineapple and kelp, I have found ripe persimmons to be not only a delicious fruit but also a beneficial aid to winning and extending throat health. The persimmons must be quite ripe. When unripe they are astringent, wholly bad-tasting, making your mouth pucker unhappily.

"But there is a further use for persimmons," I continued. "Aside from eating and enjoying ripe persimmons in the raw state, I recommend using persimmon water in the following way. Pour boiling water over a couple of persimmons and allow the water to soak up the persimmon content in this way as you let it stand until the water cools down. Then use the cooled-down persimmon water as a gargle. It offers quite fine help in sore throats and tonsillitis attacks.

"The same technique serves in many cases with garlic water. Boiling water poured over several cloves or toes of raw garlic, and then inhaling the garlic fumes *into the open mouth* acts as a direct antibiotic of the best natural variety.

"It also helps in virtually all cases of throat soreness and hoarseness to swallow a finely chopped clove or two of raw garlic with a bit of distilled water or fresh pineapple juice once or twice a day. This is using nature's own antibiotic in the most intelligent way possible. As is the case with most other natural miracle foods, here the garlic aids a large spectrum of other ills in the system."

I then reminded them of a valuable throat-healthifying technique that I had written about in several of my books and other works.

"Now here is an unbelievably easy way to build up resistance against infection and disease in the throat. All you have to do to make the muscles of the throat strong and resistant is to exercise them daily by the simple method of gargling with water and pronouncing *aloud* the vowels of the alphabet. Say A . . . E . . . I . . . O and U very loudly as you gargle. You may use any liquid you choose if you want to substitute water for something else. But if you have a tendency toward sore throat, the kind that lingers and lingers interminably after every cold, doing this will make the very muscles involved in throat problems stronger and more resistant to disease.

"This is a rather sophisticated little technique for it puts to work the exact muscles of the throat that lack resistance and get sick in people with tendencies toward sore throat. As you gargle, just to keep from swallowing the nasty stuff that you're gargling, you simply must use (and strengthen) the muscles seldom used in everyday life and therefore weak from disuse."

Timothy's wife was making notes and I knew she would take charge of her husband's health properly, for paper never forgets. It is a sheer delight to work with such people as patients or their "far better halves."

"In addition to exercising the under-exercised throat muscles every day in this way," I concluded, "I have one more little home remedy of a natural kind to give you for emergency use besides the fresh pineapple, kelp, persimmons and raw garlic. It is a drink to take when you have just begun to develop the symptoms of a cold—the kind that usually leaves a lingering sore throat in its wake."

I waited while Timothy's lady wrote down the simple recipe.

"Fill a large ten-ounce glass two-thirds full of boiling distilled water. Then add about one-third of a glass of freshly squeezed grapefruit juice. Top this with a tablespoonful or two of raw honey, according to taste. Sip this mixture s-l-o-w-l-y when you are in bed for the night, well-covered under blankets and in an airy room." I paused while Tim's wife wrote this down. "The one-third of a glass of grapefruit juice will cool down the hot water to acceptable temperature," I explained. "The heat will relax the throat tissues. The citrus juice and vitamin C in the fruit juice will tend to act as a mucus solvent, or 'cut the mucus' in the throat while the honey will soothe the irritated throat lining. As this is drunk slowly it opens the pores and sweating usually follows, which is why you must be in for the night when taking this. It is an easy and quite effective way to abort sore throats in their incipience."

When Timothy got rid of both his neck discomfort and hoarseness he fell happily back into his selling groove and never again reported to the office. But his dear wife had the goodness to telephone and say to me, "That man of mine is well, more well than he's been for years. That miracle stuff in pineapple is a big *must* around our house . . . and I give his neck a good stretch besides at bedtime whenever I think of it. Would you believe that it has been a full year that Tim's gone without a cold or any hoarse throat whatever?"

SUMMARY

Principal miracle food: RAW RIPE PINEAPPLE

Assisting miracle foods: PERSIMMONS
                                 KELP
                                 RAW GARLIC
                                 GRAPEFRUIT JUICE (fresh squeezed)
                                 RAW HONEY (small quantity)

16

Readily Obtainable
Foods That Can Add
Ten Years to Your Life

In our culture the great fear appears to be keeping from breathing air that is laden with disease-causing particulates, contaminants and pollutants, and from poisoning ourselves with carcinogenic additives, wrong foods, incompatible combinations.

The impure air causes the human system to operate in a state that is ill at ease (dis-ease), which is a drag on the respiratory apparatus of the body, also a drag on the circulatory system consequent on the halted or impeded flow of blood and other vital fluids.

The bad or contaminated foodstuffs create a drag on the digestive system, cause a pileup of uneliminated debris and toxemic waste products in the muscle fibers, the intercellular spaces, the joints, the sinuses.

Thus, any program which works in the human system to cleanse the sinus areas and the circulatory and respiratory systems of clogging blockages will almost automatically add ten years or even more to our race of upright-walking men and women.

There are such foods and such a program available. They are not usually found in conventional medical textbooks. Most of them stem from independently researched projects, not particularly encouraged by medical or pharmaceutical interests because they entail no drug-taking in any form. But they have all been tested on actual sick people, all researched under conditions of proper controls, all work beyond anything we know in the entire United States Pharmacopeia.

Here is a preliminary list of readily obtainable foods that, in all cases under study, made such healthifying changes in the followers of the program as to warrant our saying they can add at least ten years to life—especially if one is in the middle years, somewhat less if one is already elderly. But there is one other item of equal importance to adding years to life. That is the adding of good and pain-free life to those additional years. So I urge that what follows be observed as closely as conditions permit. What I say to patients who are genuinely sick and need help from the list below is this: Read and <u>Heed</u>—underscoring the "Heed" because I have found too many who read and agree with a program but then neglect to follow it.

Foremost among things to heed as you begin this program of adding ten or more years to your life is the matter of small meals. It is better to eat five or six tiny meals a day than the accustomed "three squares." The saying is not merely amusing but actually true that "Square Meals Make Round Bellies."

And also important to heed is the matter of no drinking with meals, for beverages thin down or make watery-weak the enzymes which must digest the incoming food. Thus, no beverages of any kind, no water, soda, beer, wine, coffee or tea. Soup may be spooned into the mouth with every bite of solid food if "washing down" your food is necessary.

To add years to life, table salt must be forbidden. No condiments should be taken. In a little while the real natural flavors of unseasoned foods will be tasted and appreciated.

Foods that tend to form too much aggravating mucus discharges in the body are butter, sweet and sour cream, meat fats, lard, salt, refined sugar, hard cheeses, skin of fish and fowl, whole milk, even such vegetable fats as avocado and olives. The foods named mucus solvents (because they tend to dissolve overloads of mucus in the body) are lemons, sour oranges, sour grapes, pineapple, grapefruit, limes, tomatoes and all berries—strawberries, loganberries, blackberries, blueberries, etc. Although I generally advise those with arthritis to refrain from eating citrus fruits because they often increase pains and also tend to slow one down, in cases of maxillary or frontal sinusitis they can be used in moderation as solvents of the plugged mucus in the sinus areas.

In the foods that follow, one has choices in the various classifications of those items that have tested out as the best in their divisions: the best of the protein foods, the best starchy or carbohydrate foods, the best fruits, drinks, vegetables, etc. They add years to one's life by cleaning out the plugged sinuses, by nourishing the cells, by sweeping out of the human system the clogging debris and disease-causing waste matter that hold people in bondage to sickness.

In all cases, be it remembered, these health-building foods will best be absorbed and assimilated and utilized by the body *if*—a most important *if*—you follow a program of keeping yourself in structural alignment so that the various bodily organs can perform the jobs for which they were created. Doing this is really easy; you need but follow the self-aligning drills and exercises in this book, which not only tend to release your accumulated nerve pressures (which all of us acquire in the course of living against gravity and straining at daily tasks) but also optimize your general health in most unexpected directions.

FOODS THAT ADD YEARS TO LIFE
AND LIFE TO YEARS

The <u>Read and Heed</u> List

Proteins—Wheat germ cereal, raw sunflower seeds, pumpkin seeds, sesame seeds, alfalfa (powder or tablets). Raw unsalted nuts: pecans, almonds, cashews, filberts, Brazils, walnuts, peanuts (raw, unsalted) occasionally. Red salmon, sardines packed in water, not oil, tofu (or bean curd), drumsticks of chicken or turkey without the skin or hard tissues. Mackerel and halibut, broiled or baked, without consuming the skin. Cottage cheese, skim milk occasionally, poached or soft boiled egg, the whites preferred over the yolks, and not more than two a week.

Adding to a daily bowl of wheat germ cereal such items as

lecithin flakes, brewer's yeast, bone meal, blackstrap molasses and fresh fruit is equivalent to adding life insurance.

Among the best of protein meals that do the body good and leave no toxic debris is this: Two or three ounces of raw pecans or almonds, a small slice of tofu, and a large plate of salad vegetables topped with plain yogurt and one tablespoonful of cold-pressed safflower oil. Kelp powder may be used instead of salt.

Another life-extending protein meal two or three times a week is a plate of slow-cooked soybeans. These soybeans can be mashed into a buttery spread, also they can be mixed with ground pecans, sunflower seeds and sesame seeds for extra nutritional power.

Some researchers have declared raw almonds to be so valuable that as few as two of them eaten daily will save a person from cancer. I have not tested this. But I do know that within almonds exists exactly the ingredient or organic substance that is said to provide protection against the onslaught of cancer, the same as that which is contained in apricots, and on which the controversial Laetrile treatment depends.

Other important proteins that are useful in moderate doses are peas, navy beans and lima beans. Since they tend to form intestinal gas I recommend their use less than I do soybeans with their greatly valuable lecithin content, and wheat germ, which along with bananas has in some tests of mine sustained life and health for long periods of time. Nuts such as pecans, almonds, cashews, filberts and walnuts, especially pecans and almonds, raw and unsalted, together with a raw salad plate have for many patients constituted the perfect noonday meal, one with absolutely no toxemic after-effects.

In general, foods such as the above named proteins and the citrus fruits and berries which clean out the debris from sinus areas, particularly the frontal and maxillary sinuses, also tend to nourish and rejuvenate the two organs which in our mode of civilized living chiefly get into trouble: the liver and pancreas.

Starches—Bananas, potatoes and corn. Mainly these three can add many years to one's life, while prepared starches and factory items such as breads, spaghetti, pastries and bakery products in general make for digestive problems, pileups of mucus and debris, all manner of ailments not usually traceable to inappropriate eating habits. I know I will make enemies saying this, but tests with patients have shown me that they do better without any baked goods whatever, and I have come to this opinion so firmly that I taught patients to name even their favorite bakery "The Poisoneria."

Bananas can easily become a favorite carbohydrate food. They alone can sustain life, and do for some species of monkeys. One lone ripe banana plus a ripe peach or a half pound of cherries can constitute so good a breakfast that almost anyone with whatever ailment can improve on it. Corn can be eaten raw right from the ear, and should be preferred that way. I have taught patients who never thought of eating raw corn on the cob to take it in this form and they have come to enjoy it immensely. However, cooked corn is also useful and even canned corn is valuable if unsalted. Baked or boiled potatoes represent great value and should be consumed for muscle strength and improved energy. Irish potatoes are good; yams and sweet potatoes are even better for most people.

I am not really certain whether to classify some very valuable grains as proteins or starches, for they are both in fact. Brown rice is a food I have recommended with good reason throughout the pages of this book. Whole barley, ditto. Whole grains such as oatmeal, rolled oats, cornmeal, buckwheat, and of course whole wheat and wheat germ are among the prized foods for adding years to life and life to years. Even granola, if unsugared, is a good starchy food.

When I recommend baked potatoes I also urge the use of plain (unsweetened) yogurt in place of the sour cream served in restaurants. Chives along with the yogurt are acceptable. At home a tablespoonful of cold-pressed safflower oil on the baked potato gives it additional value.

In this borderline classification I feel I should list dried fruits because they hang between being carbohydrates and proteins. Dates, dried figs, and to a lesser extent raisins, are useful in moderate amounts *if* they are sun-dried instead of hurried through sulphur fumes, and *if* one is constipated and needs a little help in this area, and *if* it is wintertime and one feels cold and is in need of additional calories.

Drinks—Bioflavonoids especially. Warm distilled water with a tablespoonful of blackstrap molasses provides iron and silicon and other extremely valuable aids to a longer, healthier life. Rice water has a variety of values and uses; see the recommendations in the chapters dealing with many serious ailments. Barley water is a drink of importance, always to be taken between meals and never at mealtimes, although the British royal family, according to one author intimate with their dining habits, claims their rosy cheeks stem from having only barley water as the favored beverage at every meal. Coconut milk, when available, is a good drink. Alfalfa tea has remarkable values and should be taken warm or cooled down from time to time. No drink should be rushed into the stomach—not guzzled, quaffed or sent down the gullet in a torrent, but sipped slowly. And no drink should be taken to "wash down" the mouthfuls chewed at mealtime, for the needed enzymes are thus watered down and less able to begin metabolizing the nutrients. If a drink is absolutely needed, a small cube of watermelon will provide the safest, cleanest fluid available anywhere. Merely take a bit of watermelon as you would a drink of any table beverage.

Tap water is not recommended, the chlorine and fluorides and other contaminants do not make for added life or years. Milk is not recommended in any form, although skim milk can be used occasionally with wheat germ as a cereal. The advertising says that, "No one ever outlives or outgrows the need for milk," but do not believe it. As soon as teeth came into your head you outgrew the need for milk, even mother's milk, for you were then able to chew more substantial fare.

Citrus fruit juices may be used occasionally, but not if you are arthritic or tend toward rheumatic or gouty problems. A desirable fruit juice can be made in a juicer or blender out of watermelon. Canteloupe, peaches or other ripe fruits can also serve. Tomato juice is allowable, and even the canned variety can be recommended if it is unsalted.

No drinks should be taken ice cold. And absolutely none should be drunk scalding hot, for they blister the mucosa that lines the throat and tests have been shown serious sequel problems, even cancer of the throat, from drinking hot beverages.

Fruits—Papaya and cherries, principally. Persimmons when

obtainable are useful in some conditions (see text). Good morning fruits are grapes, pears, peeled apples, nectarines, mangos, and of course bananas, papayas, cherries, persimmons and watermelon. As a rule melons should not be eaten along with other fruits. One researcher claims that you should eat melons alone or leave them alone. A good and safe rule is this: Combine fruits only with fruits—they do not mix well with starches or proteins. For added years and added health, become enslaved to the habit of eating a daily fruit breakfast. One can as easily become the slave of a good habit as of a bad one. After just one month of consuming only fruits for breakfast you will not be likely to want any other kind of morning nutrition.

Vegetables—Raw tomatoes, cucumbers, peppers, onions, radishes, celery and lettuce especially. Raw zucchini squash is also well received by most sick people and generally aids in gaining and retaining health. Raw spinach and all the greens—mustard greens, broccoli, turnip tops, dandelion greens, collards, comfrey, scallions, parsley—make an excellent plate taken with about a dozen pecan nuts or tofu or a couple of ounces of sunflower seeds or red salmon as a mid-day protein. As a salad dressing I advise one tablespoonful of cold-pressed safflower or soya oil plus as many spoonsful as desired of plain yogurt as a topping.

Vegetables that can be lightly steamed are cauliflower, eggplant, parsnips, all with plenty of garlic cloves for extra taste and value. Tomatoes are useful in almost any form, especially for those with diabetic backgrounds or those with simple glycosuria—sugar showing in the urine. While raw tomatoes may be best, I have in all honesty found boiled and baked and even canned whole peeled tomatoes to be of equal value, the latter if unsalted.

Raw garlic may be considered to be nature's authentic, natural antibiotic. In many cases, intelligent researchers and leaders in India take a clove or two of chopped raw garlic a few times a day and appear to conserve their health plus mental agility well into old age. In some Soviet hospitals garlic is used as an intestinal disinfectant. Raw or cooked, this is a most useful food that can add years to anyone's life.

A vegetable of great importance is asparagus. In this case canned asparagus (the spears) have been found by me to be even more valuable than the fresh variety.

HOW TO COMBINE THESE LIFE-PROLONGING FOODS INTO LIFE-PROLONGING DIETS

For good health all meals must be small meals. No exceptions allowed. It sounds contradictory, but the rule is as follows: "To eat more eat less; then you will live longer to eat more."

I can recommend a morning life-prolonging dish that helps almost every patient; it hardly matters what the ailment is. It is a fruit breakfast. Mankind grew out of fruitarianism. We were fruitarians before we even became vegetarians; that is, if life began in the tropics, where I believe it did. In tropical climes fruits were plentifully available, and that's about all our early ancestors ate, with the possible exception of a bit of fish that hardy or adventurous ones caught if they had the wit and skill to devise fishing equipment. Later, as they wandered northward where tropical fruits did not grow, people learned how to grow vegetables and became vegetarians. Still later they wandered farther north and had to learn how to hunt for meat, and their digestive apparatus adjusted to flesh proteins. In my years of doctoring in fields of natural healing I learned that if I was baffled by any patient's condition and did not know what was the matter, I could fall back on one workable technique of healing and all the sick ones improved. It was the fruit diet—returning to primordial fruitarianism.

The fruit breakfast that is a life-extending meal for very nearly everyone consists of something like this. One ripe pear, one large ripe peach, half a pound of seedless grapes. Or this combination: half a pound of cherries and a large slice of watermelon. Or, for a change, one entire melon, cantaloupe or any other type of melon, with nothing else eaten at that meal. A fourth combination of great value is just one ripe banana plus a peeled apple and a nectarine or persimmon if available.

Try any of the above fruit breakfasts for a month and note the unexpected improvement in health just from that single eating technique.

The best combination of foods is no combination at all. We all know people who complain after eating certain mixtures of foods; they belch, burp, have sour stomach complaints or gas pains, and such. Well, if they only ate a single food at any one meal, and as much as they desired of that single food, they would suffer no untoward reactions because any food they choose combines well with itself. No incompatible combinations are possible that way.

In our little coastal California city we had an elderly visitor from India who taught philosophy at the State University. Devdhar complained of chronic, unremitting fatigue, enough mental energy but no physical energy whatever. Getting the old gentleman back to normal vigor was simple, really. For three days he ate only one food at a meal, nine different foods in all for the three meals per day, all small meals. For breakfast he consumed only watermelon, for lunch only bananas, for the evening meal only an avocado, changing these to choices of a single food from among cherries, papayas, grapes and melons among fruits; boiled potato or steamed zucchini or cauliflower for a vegetable lunch; ground sunflower seeds or several raw ears of corn for the evening meal. Afterward he drank several cups of warm distilled water with a tablespoonful of blackstrap molasses stirred into each cup, taking three such cups daily. His system handled this well, absorbing the organic iron with apparent avidity. He then went to a lot of raw salad vegetables plus dried dates and combined wheat germ and sunflower seeds for protein intake, and in less than a month the old gentleman was a middle-ager full of vigor and health.

Ganish Devdhar, the old gentleman from Poona, India, was not an exception, for similar mono-diets (only one food at any one mealtime) helped many other really sick people out of their ailments. In his case I added soybeans, mashed and mixed with ground sunflower seeds as a buttery spread, and when I saw him months later he appeared more buoyant than a man thirty years younger. He became acclimated to a breakfast of wheat germ plus bananas, and a salad plus soybean spread on whole wheat toast for lunch, and this, he said, was for him a permanent open door to health.

The fruitarian diet is only one near-perfect way to health

and vigor. The mono-diet plan may be followed for as much time as one wishes, provided a good protein such as sunflower or pumpkin seeds or wheat germ is consumed as one of the daily meals.

For those who are accustomed to more luxurious diets, or who just plain like eating too much to live a Spartan existence, consider the following meals, which can add many years to the average person's life.

BREAKFASTS

Wheat germ cereal with skim milk. Add lecithin flakes and yeast.
Whole wheat toast spread thickly with soybeans-and-sunflower mash.
Warm distilled water with blackstrap molasses.
One pound of peaches or nectarines.
One peeled apple, one pear, one or two bananas.
Tall glass of fresh-squeezed carrot juice.
Six sun-dried dates if desired for extra energy.
One or two baked apples (with raw honey in cored areas) plus a warm bioflavonoid drink.
Full can of asparagus spears together with its juice in a blender for a morning pick-me-up.
Rolled oats sweetened with blackstrap molasses and/or carob powder.
Glass of warm distilled water with alfalfa tablets or powder.

LUNCHES

Two or three bananas plus two ounces of sunflower seeds.
Four ounces of fresh cabbage juice, if available.
Half an avocado.
Glass of unsalted tomato juice.
Two ears of corn eaten raw.
Boiled or baked potato with cold-pressed safflower oil instead of sour cream, plus as much plain yogurt as desired for a topping.
Two ounces of assorted raw nuts, especially pumpkin seeds if there is a prostate gland problem.
Steamed cauliflower and carrots.

Raw vegetable salad topped with yogurt and safflower oil.
Tall glass of fresh-squeezed carrot juice.

DINNERS

Entire meal consisting only of fruit, chosen from among apples,
  pears, peaches, grapes, nectarines, cherries and persimmons.
Large raw vegetable salad with yogurt and safflower or soya oil.
Two to three ounces of raw pecans and almonds, mixed.
One small helping of tofu.
Fresh vegetable soup or unsalted tomato soup, never very hot.
Raw vegetable salad.
Baked eggplant or steamed peas and carrots.
Large glass of carrot juice or unsalted tomato juice or warm water
  with tablespoonful of blackstrap molasses. If alfalfa is desired,
  as many as 12 alfalfa tablets may be added to the eight ounces
  of warm distilled water.

Note: Any of these suggested lunches or dinners may be
interchanged or transposed; that is, you may eat any of the
proposed lunchtime meals in the evening, or vice versa.

Addendum: Those with night rising or urinary problems
should take no beverages after six in the evening. The foregoing
meals would serve better for almost everyone if divided into six
small meals rather than the three large ones, and I suggest in that
case that they be eaten about two hours apart in six nearly equal
meals. Serious-minded healthseekers should avoid restaurants,
for even the best of them have at times been cited for poor
sanitation, kitchens overrun by roaches and rat droppings, etc.
The world's long-lived people eat at home rather than in restaurants, and the proper *simple* foods are obtainable at home, not
when eating out. Of first importance also for people with digestive ills and healthseekers in general is this: lay down your knife
and fork between mouthfuls, while chewing. This alone disci-
plines one to eat more slowly, chew more carefully, consume
smaller meals.

Other simple instructions that can enable most of us to add
many years to our lives are these. Stay away from smoking areas,
for some of what the smoker inhales you inhale also. Refrain

from over-proteinizing yourself—hold down the daily protein intake to no more than three ounces of nuts, wheat germ, fish, tofu, grains, cottage cheese, skim milk, whites of eggs, etc. Drink only when thirsty, for when you drink anything like morning coffee (for which almost no one arises with a real thirst), or alcoholic beverages which are socially acceptable but do not answer a genuine thirst signal in the body, you fill no physiological need and thereby insult the organism. To drink when not thirsty is like eating when not hungry—both do imponderable harm to the body. Finally—and of enormous importance—try to do at least some of the exercises and simple self-aligning drills given in these chapters every single day, for the body needs only a little daily joint movements to keep itself elastic and able to perform the jobs for which it was created.

I have not yet mentioned cabbage juice, which is a potent life-extending drink for those who tolerate it well. Four ounces sipped slowly as a morning rise-and-shine drink has helped many sick people hurry back into health. In cases of stuffy nose or congested sinus the fumes of crushed garlic have served many patients well and naturally, with no side effects. Most of us should train ourselves to use a shaker of kelp in place of the salt shaker, particularly those with thyroid problems, low energy index, failing memory and lessened sex drive. And a chlorophyll drink (made of leafy green vegetables juiced with a bit of distilled water) helps the pancreas, liver and digestive organs of every adult person, in my experience.

In general, dairy products should be avoided by those with heart dysfunctions, and by most people also. I have found that even the calcium in milk, for which milk is highly praised, is not beneficially utilized by the body after the process of pasteurization, because the degree of heat in the pasteurizing technique changes the mineral into unacceptable calcium. Also, it must be understood that it is the cream in milk that makes it mucus-forming. Skim milk, while not in my opinion a great food, is better because the harmful cream content has been skimmed off. Because of this, those who take yogurt and cheese should seek these products from non-pasteurized, or raw, milk.

SUMMARY

Principal miracle foods: BIOFLAVONOIDS (mucus solvents)
KELP
SUNFLOWER SEEDS
PECANS
BLACKSTRAP MOLASSES
ALFALFA
ALMONDS
SOYBEANS
BANANAS
PAPAYAS
CHERRIES
TOMATOES
GARLIC

Assisting miracle foods: ASPARAGUS
LECITHIN
PINEAPPLE
PERSIMMONS
CARROTS
CAULIFLOWER
EGGPLANT
RAW EARS OF CORN
GRAPES (seedless)
PEACHES
APPLES (peeled)
TOFU (bean curd)
WHEAT GERM
BROILED MACKEREL
BROILED HALIBUT
CHICKEN DRUMSTICK (no skin)

WATERMELON
DISTILLED WATER
CARROT JUICE
CABBAGE JUICE
WHEAT GERM TOAST AND SOYBEAN
  SPREAD
ROLLED OATS
BAKED POTATO
PUMPKIN SEEDS
BONE MEAL
YOGURT
SESAME SEEDS
MELONS (eaten alone)

17

Inexpensive Foods With Power to Cleanse the Human Bloodstream

The human bloodstream is self-cleansing, or almost so. It needs only a little help to cleanse and renew itself. The tendency of the entire human system is toward the normal; that is why cuts heal themselves and torn or gouged muscles go through natural repair processes without the necessity of being doctored. Whether your ailment is diagnosed, misdiagnosed or not even diagnosed at all, its tendency is to repair its own damages and get well.

There are inexpensive foods that help the system repair itself and the bloodstream cleanse itself. In the following pages there are set forth in simple terms the program that boosts the blood's ability to make itself clean and pure. But the program can be thwarted by ingesting non-foods that parade as foods. Most people with impure bloodstreams that are victims of frequent infections violate and insult their bodies daily with the kind of rubbish they throw into themselves. On these pages is written what to eat and also what to avoid, and also, very importantly, how to replace your strained and out-of-adjustment body into good structural alignment so that it can do its job of self-cleansing quickly and perfectly.

As a doctor dedicated for more than fifty years to methods of natural healing, and who has achieved successes over and over again with ailments that medical people thought irremediable or incurable, I urge you to obey the following advice and you will forever be grateful.

First of all read this book through in its entirety, regardless of your individual healthseeking goal or your particular ailment. This is important because the healing techniques overlap and many instructions for one type of ailment will cover quite another kind. Also, in reading the chapters about miracle foods for the nerves, or for the lungs or kidneys let us say, they may provide you with valuable aids for friends who have problems with their nerves or lungs or kidneys, although your own chief interest may be with a program for the urinary bladder or arthritic joints. Then, after getting acquainted with the entire book and its recommendations for all kinds of maladies, read the particular chapter that emphasizes a program for your own condition.

Only then, I am firmly convinced, should you take up the blood-cleansing program in this chapter regardless of what your own problem is. Why is this excellent advice? Because when you cleanse your bloodstream you will be augmenting the healing powers of your body. You will thus have prepared the organism to repair its damages, no matter in what organ such damages may exist. You should further resist and avoid taking on board polluted or incompatible foods such as canned or smoked meats, delicatessen temptations that hold up the healing processes by piling up waste products, coffee and cola drinks which stimulate the liver and pancreas adversely, and especially injectibles or shots which are foreign objects in the bloodstream and weaken your resistance against disease by polluting the very bloodstream upon which health depends. Then you should, in one short month, attain exciting results in renewed health, strength, ambition and clearheadedness that you had hardly expected achievable.

Here then is the preliminary pathway to health that you should paste up within constant view of your eyes.

THE PRELIMINARY EIGHT-DAY
BLOOD-CLEANSING DETOXIFICATION

For eight days you will concentrate on cleansing your blood, and such sick tissues that you may have in your body, of poisons and piled-up debris that have both debilitated the system and prevented the return to health of ailing tissues, organs, cells.

It should be borne in mind that during this eight-day program you offer the digestive system and entire body a complete physiological rest, perhaps for the first time in your life. This is utterly important because while thus resting, the body can devote its latent and potential energies to healing itself.

The eight days are divided into four two-day periods, as follows:

For the first two days you consume only watermelon and small drinks of distilled water flavored with freshly squeezed lemon juice. Every hour of the day from 8 a.m. to 8 p.m. you eat a small piece of watermelon, then one hour later drink half a cup (about 4 ounces) of distilled water with a bit of lemon it it, then another piece of watermelon on the following hour, one hour later another half cup of water-lemon drink, and so on throughout the day.

The watermelon slices should be small, weighing about two ounces. To prepare the lemon-water, mix about six ounces of fresh lemon juice with three pints of water, then drink four ounces of this every other hour of the day.

During these two days you drink nothing else and of course eat nothing at all, except psyllium seeds soaked in distilled water twice daily on the half-hour between taking the watermelon and lemon water, as explained below.

In a cup of distilled water soak one tablespoonful of any good brand of psyllium seeds for about one hour, then drink it at, say, 9:30 a.m. and again another similar dose at 5:30 p.m. This is not food, but merely provides bulk for mechanical influence on peristaltic action, ridding your body of accumulated debris as a starter for cleansing and detoxifying the bloodstream.

If watermelon is not available you may substitute four ounces of carrot juice or four ounces of canteloupe juice, but watermelon is preferred.

During this 2-day period you will very likely urinate much more than you are accustomed to, which is normal and no cause for concern.

For the second two days you consume only carrot juice and distilled water, alternating 4-ounce portions of these two drinks every hour on the hour between 8 a.m. and 8 p.m. By this time the psyllium seeds taken the first two days will usually have brought on copious bowel evacuations to rid you of accumulated surface wastes, and no more psyllium seeds are to be taken. The drinks, it should be remembered, must be slowly sipped at almost room temperature, never guzzled rapidly and never very hot or ice cold.

For ideal helpfulness to your ailing body during these first four days of the eight-day program, try to remain in bed in a dark but well-aired room. Conserve the energy usually expended by the eyes, saving this for healing purposes. I do not recommend that you utilize this time for catching up on other work, on writing letters, or listening to the radio, or other forms of expending bodily forces. For once in your life devote this one week or so to *doing nothing intelligently.* Just rest. Do nothing. Merely permit your body to heal itself, as it surely will make an effort to do with this kind of understanding cooperation from you.

If you should undergo a spell of faintness or dizziness while on this program, a matter which sometimes but not often happens, just take on your tongue a bit of raw honey or a half teaspoon of blackstrap molasses to raise the level of your blood sugar.

For the third two days your program is as follows:

On day five you take a whole orange in the morning, two hours later a whole tomato, two hours later one or two lightly steamed pieces of zucchini squash, and two hours later half a ripe grapefruit. Then repeat this throughout the day. If thirsty between the two-hour periods, on the hour drink a four-ounce portion of either carrot juice or unsalted tomato juice. At bedtime take half a cup of warm water into which you have stirred about two teabags of alfalfa tea or six tablets of alfalfa.

On day six you take four ounces of "green gold" every two hours, alternating it with four ounces of bioflavonoid drinks on the in-between hours. Thus, at 8 a.m. you have a drink of green gold (explained below), at 9:00 a bioflavonoid drink (also explained below), at 10:00 another green gold drink, at 11:00 another bioflavonoid drink, etcetera.

To make the green gold drink, pour a little distilled water into a blender and add parsley, spinach, celery, kale, lettuce, cabbage, beet tops, green peppers and other green leafy vegetables. Add raw garlic to taste; also a bit of lemon juice and a sprinkling of kelp powder. Whirl this around at high speed and you will have a beneficial, chlorophyll-rich drink of green gold.

To make the bioflavonoid drink, pour two cups of orange juice into a blender and then add the entire contents of one lemon, skin and pulp and all, cut up into small bits. Whirled at high speed this will give you a helpful blood-cleansing drink that you should learn to take with frequency even after this eight-day program.

On days seven and eight you wind up this preliminary blood-cleansing detoxification program with what is aptly called *The Mono-Diet*. Mono means just one. The mono-diet is a single food diet. Just one food at a meal, but as much as you care to eat of just the one food. At one meal you may have all the oranges you want to consume, but only oranges. Then there is no digestive trouble because the best combination is no combination at all and certainly oranges combine compatibly with themselves. At another meal you eat only bananas, as many as you like. At still another meal only nuts, or only sunflower seeds, or only soybeans, etc.

The list from which your choices can be made follows. It must be considered also, in addition to the one-food items at mealtimes, that a clove of finely chopped raw garlic drunk down with a bit of distilled water *between meals*, say, three times a day, helps mightily to disinfect an impure bloodstream and should be followed not only during the mono-diet period but ever afterwards.

CHOICES FOR MONO-DIETS

TOMATOES	CHERRIES	PEELED APPLES
BANANAS	PEACHES	CAULIFLOWER
RAW CORN	WATERMELON	PEARS
CUCUMBERS	SUNFLOWER SEEDS	AVOCADO
RAW ZUCCHINI	TOFU	PUMPKIN SEEDS
PECANS	SOYBEANS	SESAME SEEDS
BEAN SPROUTS	GRAPES	STRING BEANS
ALFALFA SPROUTS	COOKED EARS OF CORN	CARROTS (raw)
BAKED POTATOES	STEAMED ZUCCHINI	TANGERINES
STEAMED CARROTS	DATES (sun dried)	PERSIMMONS
CANTALOUPES	NECTARINES	MUSHROOMS
RAW PEANUTS	RAW ALMONDS	SWEET PLUMS
RED SALMON	CHICKEN LEGS	SARDINES
LETTUCE	CABBAGE	

A meal of only lettuce, or only a quarter head of raw cabbage, may be made by adding kelp powder for seasoning, with a dollop of plain yogurt if desired.

No salt is permitted, not even iodized salt. No vinegar, no liquors of any kind, and no carbonated drinks, or beverages much colder or hotter than room temperature. Following this eight-day program, a tablespoonful of cold-pressed safflower oil or soya oil is permitted (and encouraged) in a salad along with kelp powder and plain yogurt.

OTHER BLOOD-CLEANSING WAYS

The foregoing program is a tested and effective way for starting one on the road to health by cleansing the bloodstream in a quick and precise manner. It is admittedly rigid. For those without the desire or stamina or discipline for such rigidity, there are other ways to cleanse the bloodstream with inexpensive foods. They are extremely useful, also. One is an excellent program for those who are very stout. Another is an innovative and excitingly successful way to health for those who have bladder and kidney difficulties. Finally, there is the highly desirable Maintenance Program—one that can be recommended for everyone for all the remaining days and years of his or her life.

For the Overweight

Eat only fruit for breakfast. The choice is among oranges, grapefruits, and one quarter-pound of seedless grapes. In place of this, one highly recommended morning pick-me-up for stout people is half a can of asparagus spears blended in its own juice until it makes a frothy, zestful drink. Sip this slowly.

Eat only banana and yogurt for lunch. Have one solid banana, not too ripe, together with a four-ounce cup of plain yogurt.

Eat only a raw salad and two ounces of assorted nuts for dinner. The salad must be flavored with as much as a full tablespoonful of powdered kelp. The salad vegetables may be lettuce, tomatoes, radishes, green peppers, scallions, celery. The nuts may be raw and unsalted pecans, almonds, also some raw peanuts in lesser quantity.

For one dinner meal, only once a week, take several slices of rye krisp or wheat germ toast spread with cooked soybeans that are mashed down into a buttery spread.

The drinks may be four ounces of unsalted tomato juice or a cup of warm water with one alfalfa teabag. Between meals and at bedtime, drink down a clove of raw garlic, finely chopped, with four ounces of distilled water.

When the desired weight is reached, try the eight-day blood-cleansing diet given at the outset of this chapter. If not able to follow this, try a week of the foregoing mono-diet program, then back to this program "for the overweight," and after a week of this go back to the mono-diet for another week, alternating between the two until the desired weight loss is achieved.

For the Very Tired

To regain energy and ambition in place of your present lethargic or ambitionless state, the following power foods are recommended to enliven your circulation and strengthen your muscles.

For two days, every hour on the hour between 8 a.m. and 8 p.m. you drink four ounces of cantaloupe juice the first hour, four ounces of carrot juice the second hour, four ounces of the drink explained in previous pages that we call "green gold," then repeat the sequence of canteloupe juice, carrot juice and green gold. Continue alternating these drinks for the two-day period. Twice daily on the half hour, say at 8:30 in the morning and 4:30 in the afternoon, drink down a tablespoonful of psyllium seeds that have been soaked in distilled water for an hour or so, following this with a full glass of distilled water. Do this only for two days, discontinuing the psyllium seeds after that.

At bedtime these first two days take a full tablespoon of blackstrap molasses in four ounces of either carrot juice or distilled water.

During the next five days you take several small daily meals (say, six meals rather than three) of the following power foods to energize you rather rapidly while at the same time cleansing your bloodstream:

BANANAS	RAW GARLIC	RAW EARS OF CORN
WHEAT GERM	TOFU	SESAME SEEDS
SUN-DRIED DATES	BROWN RICE	ALMONDS
SUNFLOWER SEEDS	PECANS	APRICOTS

Meanwhile you also supercharge your system with drinks of blackstrap molasses (in four ounces of distilled water) twice a day; two to four grams (2,000–4,000 mgs) of vitamin C daily; about 800 International Units of vitamin E; at least two teaspoons of brewer's yeast daily; and at least *some* of the exercises previously given to bring your structural framework into a state of properly functioning alignment.

After a week or two of the foregoing program, or until you feel both cleansed of waste products and possessed of renewed energy, it is recommended that you try a week of the blood-cleansing program at the outset of this chapter for further brushwork on your interior plumbing, then a week or so on a mono-diet course to top off the effort at rejuvenation.

For the Night Risers

As many of my readers know, I am an aficionado of fasting and have recommended fasting techniques as the road to health when almost no other plan promised results. I am in fact putting together a book to be entitled *The Fast Fasting Way to Health* in which I will cover this vitally important subject of repairing an ailing urinary bladder and returning it to health. I say "vitally important" because all the books and studies on fasting that I am acquainted with set forth fasting as a complete physiological rest, which it is, but permit and even encourage drinking water during a fast and thus not resting the urinary apparatus at all.

What happens during a fast in the book I refer to is that the bladder in fact overworks, urinating all the time during the no-eating program. Accordingly, I realized that fasting in the ordinary way did not aid urinary or bladder problems; but when I instituted the program set forth below, the bladder difficulties nearly always ceased.

The technique is simplicity itself. Just go for two days with no drinking at all. For two days out of a lifetime really give the urinary apparatus of your body a complete rest. Allow it to catch up, by way of a rest period, and get geared into the self-repairing activities of the rest of the body. The best way to accomplish this is to eat absolutely dry foods morning, noon and night during this two-day period, as set forth below.

Your morning meal is nothing except some dry toast or rye crisp or zwieback which has been re-dried in a toaster to remove any remaining moisture. You may however moisten it with a teaspoon, but no more, of unrefined olive oil. Be sure to masticate it thoroughly, or until it is fluid in your mouth.

For lunch the complete meal is shredded wheat, or unsugared granola, or puffed wheat or millet, as much as you want of each, and here also you may use a single teaspoonful of olive oil.

Your dinner meal is exactly the same as what you had for lunch. Only the dry foods, only one teaspoonful of olive oil, but no water or other fluid of any kind. If extreme thirst assails you, the trick is to rinse out the mouth with water and spit it out after rinsing. Sometimes a quick shower in tepid water lessens the thirst.

What is remarkable here is that you continue urinating despite your not drinking. Do not be disturbed by the color of the voided urine. What should disturb you, however, is if you stop urinating entirely. If this should happen I advise you to renew drinking at once with a four-ounce portion of water or fruit juice, sipped slowly.

In the vast preponderance of urinary bladder cases just one no-drinking period of two days was enough to restore proper bladder function and halt night rising.

For a Clean-Blood Maintenance Program

Three different kinds of breakfasts serve to maintain a clean bloodstream once it has been achieved and at the same time provide energy at a high level.

1. Fruit only.
   Choice of raw peeled apples, peaches, peeled tomatoes (serving as fruit), half pound of seedless grapes, cherries, a large portion of watermelon, two or three persimmons, a variety of stewed fruit if desired, or a whole ripe cantaloupe.
2. Bananas with yogurt
   Fresh fruit may be added to the deep dish of plain yogurt with sliced bananas: peaches, ripe pears, etc.
3. Wheat germ cereal with skim milk.
   Add two tablespoonsful of lecithin flakes, one of brewer's yeast, one teaspoonful of bone meal, fresh fruit if desired. Warm distilled water with tablespoonful of blackstrap molasses.

Lunch is preferably the protein meal of the day. Also, it is the easiest to take, considering those who consume it away from home and must take it along to work. It should provide about 50 grams of protein, but no more—and on this ration both the liver and pancreas should last a long and healthy lifetime.

1. Chicken leg with whole wheat or wheat germ bread.
   A half dozen raw pecans or four almonds.
   A half dozen sun-dried dates.
   Four ounces of unsalted tomato juice or distilled water.

2. Two to three ounces of sunflower seeds plus whole wheat or wheat germ bread, or rye crisp, and a whole peeled cucumber to serve as a drink.

3. Sandwiches of wheat germ bread spread with mashed soybeans mixed with ground sunflower and sesame seeds.
   Ten or twelve raw pecan nuts.
   One peeled cucumber or two ripe tomatoes to serve as a drink.

The evening meal should be free of protein items but have a large variety of raw salad greens and, if desired, one or two lightly steamed vegetables.

1. Large salad topped with one tablespoonful of cold-pressed safflower oil and an ounce or two of plain yogurt. Season with kelp powder if desired.
   Steamed cauliflower, zucchini squash, Irish or sweet potato if desired.
   One or two ears of raw corn on the cob.
   Drink of water, cool or warm, with tablespoon of blackstrap molasses.

2. Vegetable salad and tomato or corn soup.

3. Vegetable salad with mushrooms, raw corn, baked potato topped with yogurt and powdered kelp.

If convenient, the lunch and dinner meals may be reversed. At bedtime an extra four ounces of distilled water or carrot juice with a little blackstrap molasses is advised especially if you are a poor sleeper. Between-meal snacks should be a choice of these: orange or tangerine, pecans or almonds, sunflower or sesame seeds. If you have prostate gland trouble the better choice is pumpkin seeds as a snack and as the best protein in your case.

BLOOD-WASHING AWAY BOILS
AND CARBUNCLES

Ever since World War II Leonard had been plagued by an outbreak of carbuncles in the most undesirable places at the most undesirable times. As an accountant who sat most of his working hours, the painful nodes on his buttocks that as often as not oozed pus and needed sterile dressings, gave the desperate man a fit.

It was of course a bloodstream syndrome that required a radical bloodwashing and blood-cleansing approach. Leonard thought he had consumed poisonous foods or drinks during the war, and that these had somehow remained and even piled up in his system. Over the back of his neck and on his upper spine and especially on the cheeks of both buttocks he had red areas which covered deep, painful, pus-containing crypts. At times a siege of carbuncles would start up a fever and almost completely knock him out. We ruled out diabetes, which is sometimes a causative factor, and then went to work on a blood-cleansing program.

For half a week Leonard ate nothing but watermelon in tiny pieces, each little cube of watermelon popped into his mouth every five minutes or so. This made the man urinate so much he wondered where the buckets of fluid came from. For the next four days of the first week Leonard alternated every two hours between a spoonful of psyllium seeds in a glass of distilled water and a full eight-ounce glass of carrot juice. This continued the bloodwashing process while also giving the man more copious bowel evacuations than he had ever before experienced.

During the week of this diet plus a daily walking program the man lost 12 pounds, trimming down to just about normal weight. Then he began replacing the lost body fluids with better liquids. Every day on the hour Leonard sipped four ounces of unsalted tomato juice, distilled water, watermelon juice, carrot juice, and cantaloupe juice, rotating them in convenient order. Between the drinks on the hour he ate on the half hour such blood-cleansing foods as tomatoes, seedless grapes, cherries, bioflavonoids, as-paragus, avocado, zucchini squash, fresh ripe fruit such as peaches, nectarines, sweet plums, and sweet oranges. For bowel activity and to replenish his bloodstream with good cell-building materials, he began each day with a dish of wheat germ to which was added a little lecithin flakes, blackstrap molasses, brewer's yeast and a small spoon of powdered bone meal. At night he ended the program with a full clove or two of raw garlic swallowed with four ounces of yogurt.

Leonard gained enormous energy and doubted that what he ate could have supplied it. It was, of course, the cleansing of the blood and the start-up of self-healing in the body that brought this about.

By the second week Leonard was ready for really solid food. To lay in the proper nutritional cell-building material he ate a daily three-ounce portion of mashed soybeans, and in this form he could spread the soybeans of buttery consistency on high-fiber whole wheat or wheat germ bread. As a change of protein fare he was allowed small portions of raw pecan nuts, red salmon, sunflower or sesame or pumpkin seeds, almonds, bean sprouts and alfalfa sprouts, and chicken legs eaten without the skin. Meanwhile he spread in liberal quantities wheat germ oil on all the carbuncle-prone areas.

The results were something to marvel at. Despite the stains on bedsheets and clothing caused by the wheat germ oil, both Leonard and his wife were ecstatic. The red spots dried up and seemed to evaporate away. There appeared to be no more pus forming anywhere in his body, certainly not in the formerly favored areas.

When Leonard's skin cleared, that was the end of it. In great glee he informed me two months later that he felt renewed.

"My blood and my inside plumbing seem to be perfect," he told me. "You must be in the insurance business, Dr. Morrison, because you've certainly sold me a large hunk of life insurance."

When I called Leonard some years later on a tax matter, he reported not ever noticing "the least scintilla of a carbuncle" since the program washed his bloodstream and built into his body a high degree of resistance to infection.

ERADICATING HALITOSIS QUICKLY

Lucille had told me that during most of the 30 years she had given piano lessons she avoided getting too close to her pupils because of halitosis.

Lifelong constipation also had been a major worry in her life. At one time she thought her bowel movements were "regular" because she had BMs every three or four days regularly. Then they slowed to about once a week. Finally she read about colonic irrigations and resorted to almost daily enemas. But the bad breath, which she consistently referred to as "my halitosis" persisted until we placed her on a proper, natural, blood-cleansing get-well program.

She was told "*washing out the bowels*" *by way of enemas was not natural or desirable.*

"*The bowel is a self-cleansing organ,*" *I explained,* "*and it no more needs artificial washes than your nose needs sprays or your eyes need eyedrops.*" *She agreed at once, but wondered about her halitosis.*

"*Will it go away if I get to have normal bowel evacuations?*" *I told her I thought it would and we began the job of renewing the chemistry of her bloodstream.*

Lucille was not permitted to consume any white flour or white sugar at all, or to buy the "*convenience junk foods*" *she was accustomed to having. The lifelong constipation was easy to correct. Merely a good heaping daily dish of high-fiber cereals such as wheat germ, bran, shredded wheat or grape nuts –or all of them mixed into one breakfast dish, plus a lot of fresh fruit which was also high in roughage–this did the job rather quickly when she stopped eating sugar and white flour and junk foods.*

The bad breath left more slowly, merely lessening but not disappearing. Then she went on the mono-diet program and the halitosis business was gone. For one full week Lucille ate 21 different foods, just one food, and all she wanted of that one food, three times a day for seven days. In the morning she had all the oranges she desired, then at noon as much yogurt as she cared to swallow, and in the evening a large plate of steamed zucchini squash, for example. The next day it would be grapefruits in the morning, bananas for lunch and tofu (bean sprouts) for dinner. In this way she went through the consumption of peaches at one meal, sunflower seeds at another, cottage cheese at a third, etc.

The whole thing had gone a mere three weeks. At the end of that time her tongue was not furry and white; it was a clean red.

"*I can come close to you or anyone now,*" *she said.* "*My breath is unhalitosed.*" *And indeed it was.*

FREEDOM FROM GERM WORRY

The self-aligning exercises previously explained in earlier chapters must be done on a regular basis. As you go along, and as you feel growing energy levels, increase the time and vigor you put into the exercise drills. But do not stop doing them, else

there's a chance of cardiac decompensation and grave conse-
quences. Even on a holiday away from home, some or nearly all
of the exercises can be attended to as a morning duty—your way
of "paying dues" to your body for its giving you good health. I
stress all this because the system may be incapable of utilizing the
values in the miracle foods set forth in these pages if it is not in
such a state of alignment that the various organs can do the jobs
they were created to do, and the exercises can keep you in the
desired state of alignment.

A word about mental health seems appropriate. Do not
spend time worrying about hordes of microorganisms waiting
out there to attack you and implant a disease into your vitals. The
whole germ business does not stand up on sane and meticulous
analysis. I recall being asked by a worried patient who was an
arrested tubercular about the dependability of the miracle food
maintenance program.

"Will eating these foods and keeping my body in workable
alignment protect me against a recurrence of tuberculosis?" he
asked with deep concern. "I constantly worry about another
invasion of those tubercle bacilli which cause tuberculosis."

"Think it through and you'll not worry," I told him. "This
bacterium, the tubercle bacillus, co-exists with tuberculosis but
does not cause it. If it caused tuberculosis, then all your family or
fellow workers exposed to this organism would also have tuberculosis. What causes a sickness is lack of resistance to the
onslaught of a disease. When your lung tissue breaks down it
provides food for these bacilli, and they are found in tuberculosis. Blaming them for the disease is the "illogic" of children.
It's like blaming flies for the garbage that attracts them. If germs,
rather than lack of resistance to sickness, caused disease then our
ancestors who existed blissfully in clouds of germs would have
perished and we would not be here to discuss it. You don't see
dogs nibbling on a pile of lettuce leaves because that's not their
food. You never see horses at a pile of meat or bones because that
is not their type of food. You do see the tubercle bacillus in
tuberculosis because that kind of lung tissue is what they live on.
They co-exist with tuberculosis, they don't cause it. So worry
about keeping up your resistance against disease by way of the
sure, two-pronged approach to health: one, miracle foods that

make for health and longevity, and two, maintaining your body in structural alignment so that the miracle foods can be utilized. Beyond that, only this reminder: *Worrying in advance of an event is like paying interest on a note before it falls due."*

SUMMARY

Principal miracle foods: WATERMELON
CARROT JUICE
LEMON AND DISTILLED WATER
CANTALOUPE JUICE
UNSALTED TOMATO JUICE
SOYBEAN SPREAD
RAW PECANS
RAW WHEAT GERM
WHEAT GERM OIL
RAW GARLIC
LECITHIN FLAKES
LECITHIN LIQUID
BREWER'S YEAST
BONE MEAL
ALFALFA
RAW ALMONDS
SUNFLOWER SEEDS
SESAME SEEDS
PUMPKIN SEEDS
SUN-DRIED DATES
SEEDLESS GRAPES
YOGURT
BLACKSTRAP MOLASSES
"GREEN GOLD"
RED SALMON
KELP
CHERRIES
PSYLLIUM SEEDS

Assisting miracle foods: ZUCCHINI
         TOMATOES
         MUSHROOMS
         AVOCADO
         SAFFLOWER OIL (cold-pressed)
         UNREFINED OLIVE OIL
         BIOFLAVONOIDS
         ASPARAGUS
         BEAN SPROUTS
         CHICKEN LEGS
         SARDINES
         POTATO (Irish and sweet)
         CUCUMBERS
         GREEN PEPPERS
         CELERY
         LETTUCE
         RADISHES
         RAW PEANUTS (occasionally)
         KALE
         PARSLEY
         SPINACH
         NECTARINES
         SWEET PLUMS
         BANANAS
         SCALLIONS
         CAULIFLOWER (steamed)
         RAW CORN (on the cob)
         CARROTS (steamed)
         ONIONS (raw and boiled)
         EGGPLANT
         STRING BEANS
         VITAMINS E, C AND B

18

The Richest of Mineral-Rich Foods for Healthifying Your Body

In order to achieve the highest level of health that it is possible for you to gain and maintain you are advised to avoid drinking tap water. But you may be worried that you will thus rob the system of the minerals in water that it needs, so here are the foods that are the richest and purest of all known suppliers of the various essential minerals. By daily consumption of the foods listed in this chapter you will be purchasing a high form of life insurance because you will be giving your body the gift of all the minerals it needs in the best, richest, most utilizable manner possible, far better than the minerals of dubious quality that come to you from the ordinary tap.

CALCIUM (Needed in building bones and teeth, for clotting blood and heart action and soothing irritated nerves)

Best and easily available sources:
BONE MEAL
DOLOMITE
YOGURT
SESAME SEEDS
LEAFY VEGETABLES

MAGNESIUM (Makes calcium appropriable. Needed to regulate body heat, give strength to bones, relieve weakness and cramps)

> Best and easily available sources:
> WHOLE WHEAT
> SOYBEANS
> WHOLE GRAIN CEREALS
> RAW PECANS OR ALMONDS

ZINC (Needed for fertility and resistance to infection)

> SUNFLOWER SEEDS
> WHEAT GERM
> ASPARAGUS
> RAW NUTS
> LEAFY VEGETABLES

COPPER (Needed for weak bones, hair loss, skin rashes, cardiac weakness, and works with iron to make red blood cells)

> PEAS
> RAW NUTS
> SUN-DRIED RAISINS

IRON (Necessary for blood-making, for conveying oxygen, for fatigue and tendency toward anemia)

> BLACK MOLASSES
> KELP

IODINE (Useful in low blood pressure cases, tiredness with goitre growth, slow pulse and anemia)

> MACKEREL
> TURNIP GREENS
> CHARD
> KELP

FLUORIDE (Better than fluorides in dental use or in toothpastes which can cause brittle teeth and ugly mottling of teeth even in youth)

ALMONDS

BEET GREENS

CARROTS

SELENIUM (Goes along with vitamin E to balance sexual functions, aids in providing muscular strength, protects against liver damage)

WHOLE WHEAT CEREAL

ROLLED OATS

PHOSPHORUS (Useful in great weight loss, insufficient growth and under-mineralized bones, fatigue, poor thinking ability)

SUNFLOWER SEEDS

SESAME SEEDS

SUN-DRIED DATES

POTASSIUM (Necessary for normal heart function, paralysis, heart damage, muscular weakness, constipation, tendency to retain fluids)

MACKEREL

HALIBUT

KELP

BRAN

ALL FRUITS

CHLORIDE (Chlorides have capacity for extracting the "odor particle" that has been called "the raw stuff of cancer" from the nuclei of cancer cells)

KALE

TOMATOES

KELP

CELERY

TURNIPS

MANGANESE (Needed for digestive enzymes, fat conversion and blood formation)

WHEAT GERM CEREAL

GREEN LEAFY VEGETABLES

MOLYBDENUM (Needed in manufacture of enzymes and for oxygenation)

BREWER'S YEAST

WHOLE GRAIN CEREALS

SULPHUR (Necessary for cells of skin, nails and hair and for energy production)

SOYBEANS

KALE

SODIUM (Used in transmission of nerve impulses; tends to cause fluid retention in body)

CEREALS

KELP

DRY CEREALS

Index